T5-DHA-655

Applying English To Your Career
A Writing Manual

Deborah Davis, Ph.D.
Professor, Kaplan University

Elizabeth G. Donnellan, M.Ed.
Instructor, Kaplan University

PEARSON
Prentice
Hall

Upper Saddle River, New Jersey 07458

© 2006 by PEARSON EDUCATION, INC.
Upper Saddle River, New Jersey 07458

All rights reserved

10 9 8 7 6 5 4 3

ISBN 0-13-192115-0

Printed in the United States of America

Table of Contents

Introduction

Applying English to Your Career is an English manual designed to help you. Specifically, it is written to provide opportunities for you to practice, through career oriented exercises,

- the writing process to produce clearer college essays and papers,

- writing techniques in the nine rhetoric writing styles to learn how each applies to your career,

- punctuation and grammar skills to learn how punctuation informs the reader of your meaning in college essays and workplace writing.

Unlike other English text exercises, this manual is written to provide you with an abundant amount of exercises to practice those skills which you will need in your career. It is designed to be used in the present for practical application in the future.

This manual is unique for many reasons:

- You can focus on those areas you need to strengthen. For example, if you struggle with the use of commas, you can devote particular attention to the comma exercises in the punctuation section.

- All exercises are tailored to students studying career specific disciplines: Allied Health, AutoCAD, Automotive Technology, Criminal Justice, Electronics, Information Technology, and Paralegal Studies.

- You are provided with information regarding the relationship of the material to your career. For example, Chapter 3 (Logical Connections) shows you how to use this writing style in your workplace.

- The topics in this manual focus on career oriented student writing weaknesses and address their specific writing needs. (See the list of topics in the Table of Contents).

- You can check your responses to each exercise by comparing your answers to the provided Answer Key in the back of the manual.

This manual is designed to be used with your English text to strengthen your written communication skills so that you can be more proficient in the workplace.

Part I
The Writing Process

Chapter 1
Writing Methodologies

Prewriting

⟨ EXERCISE 1.1 ⟩

Choose a topic listed below. As explained in your text, practice the pre-writing technique of "brainstorming." Remember, make a list of whatever comes to your mind about that topic without judging or altering your ideas. Write without stopping.

Allied Health

Asepsis, bacteriostatic, endodontic, affective domain, alternative medicine, anemia, bloodborne pathogens, chronic illness, code of ethics, DNR order, homeopathy, independent practice associations, nonsteroidal anti-inflamatory drugs, passive euthanasia, phlebotomy, preferred provider organization, primary health care, reflexology, standards of clinical nursing practice, stimulus-based stress model, variance

AutoCAD

Plot, zoom, template drawing, polar array, object snap, drawing polygons, isometric drawing, drawing splines, attributes, multiple tiled viewpoints, ROTATE command, TRIM command, CHAMFER

Automotive Technology

Ackerman principle, aramid, ball socket assembly, baud rate, coefficient of friction, dof tracking, electromagnetic induction, fiber optics, fusible link, Hooke's Law, kinetic energy, MacPherson strut, Piezoelectric Principle, positive crankcase ventilation

Criminal Justice

ADMAX, adversarial system, battered women's syndrome, circumstantial evidence, civil liability, conflict perspective, fixed sentencing, due process, jural postulates, juvenile justice agency, mediation committee, *nolo contendere*, plea bargaining, probable cause

Electronics

Coulomb's law, effective value, Faraday's law, harmonics, Kirchoff's voltage law, Lenz's law, negative feedback, Ohm's law, semiconductor, terminal equivalency, troubleshooting

Information Technology

Broadband, centralized communication, communications infrastructure, computer aided systems engineering, computer-integrated manufacturing, content aggregator, consumer response supply-chain strategy, database administrator, enterprise information system, fractal method, heterogeneous application, LAN, NOS, partitioning, SAN, SMDS

Paralegal Studies

Civil law, case law, defendant, equity, felony, legal assistant, misdemeanor, personal property, power of attorney, tort, will

❖ *EXERCISE 1.2* ❖

Choose another topic from the above list. Practice the pre-writing technique of "freewriting." Freewrite for five full minutes without stopping. Do not judge or alter what you write—JUST WRITE without stopping.

❖ *EXERCISE 1.3* ❖

Find one more topic from the above list that appeals to you. Apply the "clustering" technique as explained in your book. Begin with the chosen word in the center of the page, circle it, then branch out with other words, drawing lines to and circles around the new words. Let your mind move in all directions as the cluster does. Do not judge or alter your ideas; let them flow.

ESSAY STRUCTURE

College essays should adhere to a very particular structure utilizing specific components such as a Thesis Statement, Topic Sentences, Organizing Principles, Paragraph Structures, and Transitional Phrases. Below are exercises which allow you to practice information presented in your text.

Thesis Statement

⟨⟩ *EXERCISE 1.4* ⟨⟩

Write a Thesis Statement for each of the sentences below (in your area) using the "thesis statement listing points" as discussed in your text. For example,

> **Chronic illness has affected the American workforce in adverse ways (thesis): <u>lost work hours</u> (point 1), <u>continued poor health on the job</u> (point 2), <u>and serious psychological problems</u> (point 3).**

Allied Health

1. To earn the most money working in a hospital, you need _____, _____, and _____.

2. It is important for all health care workers to wash hands frequently because _____ _____, _____, and _____.

3. Emergency workers need to update training annually because_____, _____,and _____.

4. Women should stop smoking cigarettes during pregnancy because _____, _____,and _____.

5. The MRI machine is a critical and necessary machine because _____, _____,and _____.

AutoCAD

1. The 3D model for this project indicates many possibilities for improvement, such as_____ _____, _____,and _____.

2. Adding a slope to this yard is best for this design because _____, _____,and _____.

3. It is important to update rendering programs often because _____,
   _____, and _____.

4. The plans for this sundeck are not practical because_____,
   _____, and _____.

5. We are unable to provide you with the kind of house design you want because _____
   _____, _____, and _____.

Automotive Technology

1. I think you should consider replacing the transmission because _____,
   _____, and _____.

2. Your car needs new windshield wipers; you'll need them when_____,
   _____, and _____.

3. I am ready to leave my job and open my own garage now because _____,
   _____, and _____.

4. Owning a hybrid car is (is not) preferable because_____,
   _____, and _____.

5. Owning your own service station can be a challenge because _____,
   _____, and _____.

Criminal Justice

1. The threat of terrorism is high now because _____,
   _____, and _____.

2. Being an animal control officer is (is not) a rewarding job because _____,
   _____, and _____.

3. This intersection is dangerous because _____,
   _____, and _____.

4. Wearing a protective vest can be valuable because_____,
   _____, and _____.

5. Officers need annual training in effective methods of handling domestic violence calls
   because _____, _____, and
   _____.

Electronics

1. It can be dangerous for a lineman to work in storm conditions because_____
   _____, _____,
   and_____.

2. I think it is better to work with a contracting team than alone because_____
_____, _____, and _____.

3. Wiring this apartment complex will be a difficult job because_____,
_____, and _____.

4. This downed power line can create such serious hazards as_____,
_____, and _____.

5. It is (not) better to work as a contractor than for someone else because_____
_____, _____,and _____.

Information Technology

1. In my opinion, laptops are not better computers than desktops because _____
_____, _____, and _____.

2. Every computer should have at least two USB ports because _____,
_____, and_____.

3. New DVD-ROM drives should replace the CD-ROM drive if_____,
_____, or _____.

4. It is important for information technologists to continue training in new software programs
since _____, _____, and
_____.

5. Security systems on computers (spyware and firewall protection) are essential because
_____, _____, and _____.

Paralegal

1. Mr. Smith deserves full compensation for his injuries due to_____,
_____,and _____.

2. The verdict of guilty was wrong; he was innocent due to _____,
_____,and _____.

3. I deserve a promotion in this law firm because_____,
_____,and _____.

4. I am unable to complete my paper due in torte class because _____,
_____,and _____.

5. I believe it's (not) important to volunteer for a community legal assistance center in my
community because_____, _____,
and _____.

Using the topic you chose from your Thesis Statement exercises above, develop a "thesis statement without points" as described in your text. Remember, state your idea simply and concisely-without points. For example,

> **Investing my own money to open a repair shop will prove difficult and challenging, but it is something I've always wanted to do.**

Allied Health

_____

_____

AutoCAD

_____

_____

Automotive Technology

_____

_____

Criminal Justice

_____

_____

Electronics

_____

_____

Information Technology

_____

_____

Paralegal Studies

_____

_____

Topic Sentence

A Thesis Statement gives the essay an overall direction and impression of the paper to the reader by listing points. The Topic Sentence extends that function by developing each of the points (listed in the Thesis Statement) in the body paragraphs. Paragraph topic sentences, combined with your Thesis Statement generally make up what is called the "Introduction" to your essay. As you complete the exercise below, you will see the Introduction developing.

⟨ EXERCISE 1.6 ⟩

Examine EXERCISE 4 in this chapter. Write the Thesis Statement. Below, write each point. Then, create a supporting sentence to expand each point (Topic Sentence). For example,

Thesis Statement:	This downed power line can create serious hazards such as
Point 1:	fire,
Supporting Sentence	Electrical sparks from the downed power line can create a potentially serious fire.
Point 2:	possible electrocution,
Supporting Sentence	If you touch a downed power line, you run the danger of harming yourself because of the live electricity.
Point 3:	loss of electrical power,
Supporting Sentence	A downed power line usually means no electricity in your home and perhaps in your whole neighborhood.

Allied Health

Thesis Statement: _____

Point 1: _____

  Supporting _____

  Sentence _____

Point 2: _____

  Supporting _____

  Sentence _____

Point 3: _____

  Supporting _____

  Sentence _____

AutoCAD

Thesis Statement: _____

Point 1: _____

   Supporting _____

   Sentence _____

Point 2: _____

   Supporting _____

   Sentence _____

Point 3: _____

   Supporting _____

   Sentence _____

Automotive Technology

Thesis Statement: _____

Point 1: _____

   Supporting _____

   Sentence _____

Point 2: _____

   Supporting _____

   Sentence _____

Point 3: _____

   Supporting _____

   Sentence _____

Criminal Justice

Thesis Statement: _____

Point 1: _____

   Supporting _____

   Sentence _____

Point 2: _____

   Supporting _____

   Sentence _____

Point 3: _____

   Supporting _____

   Sentence _____

Electronics

Thesis Statement: _____

Point 1: _____

    Supporting _____

    Sentence _____

Point 2: _____

    Supporting _____

    Sentence _____

Point 3: _____

    Supporting _____

    Sentence _____

Information Technology

Thesis Statement: _____

Point 1: _____

    Supporting _____

    Sentence _____

Point 2: _____

    Supporting _____

    Sentence _____

Point 3: _____

    Supporting _____

    Sentence _____

Paralegal Studies

Thesis Statement: _____

Point 1: _____

    Supporting _____

    Sentence _____

Point 2: _____

    Supporting _____

    Sentence _____

Point 3: _____

    Supporting _____

    Sentence _____

Organizational Principles

⟨ EXERCISE 1.7 ⟩

Organizing your paper is a critical element in helping the reader understand what you're saying. Based on your textbook discussion of organizing principles, develop a Thesis Statement and Topic Sentences for one of the sentences below, then organize your ideas according to the order stated.

1. What skills are necessary in your profession?

2. Where do you hope to be in five years in your profession?

3. What are employers looking for in your profession?

4. What does it take to get the kind of job you want?

Emphatic Order (greater to lesser, most to least important)

Thesis Statement: _____

Topic Sentence (most important idea) _____

_____

Topic Sentence (second most important idea) _____

_____

Topic Sentence (least important idea) _____

_____

Reverse Emphatic Order (lesser to greater, least to most important idea)

Thesis Statement: _____

Topic Sentence (least important idea) _____

_____

Topic Sentence (second most important idea) _____

_____

Topic Sentence (most important idea) _____

_____

Alternating Order (placing weaker points between two strong ones). Choose one.

1. What college courses do you think will be the most challenging?

2. What challenges do you think you'll face in your chosen career?

3. **Why did you choose the profession you did?**

4. **What can you do to help yourself through the academic process?**

Thesis Statement: _____

Topic Sentence (strong point)_____

_____

Topic Sentence (weak point) _____

_____

Topic Sentence (strong point)_____

_____

Chronological Order (time order or order of sequence) choose one.

1. **If you won the lottery, what would you do?**

2. **What steps do you take to prepare yourself for your day?**

3. **If you had an entire day to spend any way you wanted, what would you do?**

4. **How did you become involved in a hobby you have?**

Thesis Statement: _____

Topic Sentence 1_____

_____

Topic Sentence 2_____

_____

Topic Sentence 3_____

_____

Paragraph Structure

Essays follow a paragraph structure using an Introduction, Body, and Conclusion. The exercises above helped you to develop your Introduction (Thesis Statement plus Topic Sentences). The Body of your essay contains paragraphs which expand each of your main points in the Thesis Statement. In other words, each of your Topic Sentences (taken from each of the points in your Thesis Statement in the Introduction) can then be developed into full paragraphs. In addition, each paragraph contains its own Topic Sentence and refers to the Thesis Statement in the Introduction. Topic sentences usually provide transitions from one paragraph to the next.

Body

☙ *EXERCISE 1.8* ☙

Each of the incomplete sentences below expands the Topic Sentence above it. Complete and expand the sentences to further develop the Topic Sentence.

1. For me, attending college will offer me the opportunity to advance my career, secure a better paying job, and be a role model for my children.
   a. Going to college will help me in my career by _____.
   b. I know a college degree will improve my chances to make a better salary by

   _____.

   c. By going to college, my children_____.

2. I'm trying to learn the skills of time management; it's a difficult task because of my many responsibilities such as work, raising my children, and going to school.
   a. Managing my time is hard with my work schedule which _____

   _____.

   b. Not only does work take time, but my children_____

   _____.

   c. Budgeting my time includes school which _____.

3. My goal, once I get my degree, is to own my own business, so that I can be financially independent, be my own boss, and make my family proud.
   a. With my own business, I can _____.
   b. Financial independence will allow me to_____.
   c. As the owner of my own business, my family_____

   _____.

4. I'd like to learn how to reduce my stress because my blood pressure is too high, my temper flares up, and I'm not sleeping well.
   a. My high blood pressure due to stress makes my body _____

   _____.

   b. When I'm really stressed, my temper _____.
   c. Because of stress, I'm not sleeping well, so I _____

   _____.

5. In preparing for a test, I need to study several days before the test, meet with my study group, and know what will be on the test.

    a. The benefits of studying several days before the test, versus cramming the night before include _____.

    b. My study group can help me prepare for a test by_____

    _____.

    c. I need to know what will be on the test so that I can _____

    _____.

6. I know that to study efficiently, I need to create my own study place, have privacy, and regulate my study times.

    a. By creating my own study area, I can _____.

    b. Privacy when I study will help me to _____.

    c. Setting specific study times will allow me to _____.

7. To make the most out of my college education, I need to communicate with the staff, get to know my faculty advisor, and learn about my program in the college catalogue.

    a. The college staff can help me to _____.

    b. I need to know my faculty advisor because_____.

    c. The more familiar I am with the college catalogue, the more _____

    _____.

8. It's so difficult to meet new people in college. Sometimes I feel self-conscious, like no one will understand me, and that I'm so different.

    a. My being self-conscious makes me _____.

    b. I don't think any of these students will understand me because _____

    _____.

    c. I'm not like any of these students. I'm _____.

9. Taking effective notes in class will help me to better prepare for tests, understand the material, and develop my listening skills.

    a. I know the teacher asks questions on tests based on her lectures. If I take better notes, I can _____.

    b. Reviewing my notes from class helps me understand the material the teacher discussed, so taking good notes _____.

    c. Listening is so important, especially in class. It_____

    _____.

10. Writing good college papers requires knowing what the teacher wants, good grammar skills, and strong organizational skills.

   a. I have to know what the teacher wants before I write a paper, so I need to know

       _____.

   b. I know I can improve my grammar skills to write a better paper if I

       _____.

   c. Paying attention to organization in my college writing will help me to

       _____.

Transitional Phrases

Transitional phrases are those words and phrases which contribute to the paper's coherence. These phrases provide strong, solid connections between ideas and paragraphs. Transitional words act as signposts, direct the reader where you want him to go. Without them, the paper lacks unity and coherence.

❧ EXERCISE 1.9 ❧

Using the ten sentences below, add the appropriate transitional word or phrase to help the reader understand what you're saying. For example,

I know that my own study space is essential for my success. I can create my own study space by finding a place in my house I can call my own, one that is used solely for studying, and allows for necessary privacy.

     a. <u>First</u> (transitional word), I need to have a space that is all mine, not my family's, just mine.

     b. <u>In addition</u> (transitional words), I need a study place that is used exclusively for studying.

     c. <u>Finally</u> (transitional word), I need privacy for efficient studying.

1. For me, attending college will offer me the opportunity to advance my career, secure a better paying job, and be a role model for my children.

   a. Going to college will help me in my career by _____.

   b. I know a college degree will improve my chances to make a better salary by

       _____.

   c. By going to college, my children_____.

2. I'm trying to learn the skills of time management; it's a difficult task because of my many responsibilities such as work, raising my children, and going to school.
   a. Managing my time is hard with my work schedule which _____

   _____.

   b. Not only does work take time, but my children _____

   _____.

   c. Budgeting my time includes school which _____.

3. My goal, once I get my degree, is to own my own business, so that I can be financially independent, be my own boss, and make my family proud.
   a. With my own business, I can _____.
   b. Financial independence will allow me to_____.
   c. As the owner of my own business, my family _____

   _____.

4. I'd like to learn how to reduce my stress because my blood pressure is too high, my temper flares up, and I'm not sleeping well.
   a. My high blood pressure due to stress makes my body _____

   _____.

   b. When I'm really stressed, my temper _____.
   c. Because of stress, I'm not sleeping well, so I _____

   _____.

5. In preparing for a test, I need to study several days before the test, meet with my study group, and know what will be on the test.
   a. The benefits of studying several days before the test, versus cramming the night before include _____.
   b. My study group can help me prepare for a test by_____

   _____.

   c. I need to know what will be on the test so that I can _____

   _____.

6. I know that to study efficiently, I need to create my own study place, have privacy, and regulate my study times.
   a. By creating my own study area, I can _____.
   b. Privacy when I study will help me to _____.
   c. Setting specific study times will allow me to _____.

7. To make the most out of my college education, I need to communicate with the staff, get to know my faculty advisor, and learn about my program in the college catalogue.

    a. The college staff can help me to _____.

    b. I need to know my faculty advisor because_____.

    c. The more familiar I am with the college catalogue, the more _____

    _____.

8. It's so difficult to meet new people in college. Sometimes I feel self-conscious, like no one will understand me and that I'm so different.

    a. My being self-conscious makes me _____.

    b. I don't think any of these students will understand me because _____

    _____.

    c. I'm not like any of these students. I'm _____.

9. Taking good notes in class will help me to better prepare for tests, understand the material, and develop my listening skills.

    a. I know the teacher asks questions on tests based on her lectures. If I take better notes, I can _____.

    b. Reviewing my notes from class helps me understand the material the teacher discussed, so taking good notes _____.

    c. Listening is so important, especially in class. It_____

    _____.

10. Writing good college papers requires knowing what the teacher wants, good grammar skills, and strong organizational skills.

    a. I have to know what the teacher wants before I write a paper, so I need to know_____

    _____.

    b. I know I can improve my grammar skills to write a better paper if I _____

    _____.

    c. Paying attention to organization in my college writing will help me to _____

    _____.

Conclusion

The conclusion (summary) of your paper brings what you've written to a close. For most college students, the summary is used most frequently to conclude an essay; it recaps the main points of your essay using different words than in the paper.

Create a summary paragraph for three of the ten items in Exercise 1.9.

1. _____.

_____

_____

_____

_____

2. _____.

_____

_____

_____

_____

3. _____.

_____

_____

_____

_____

REVISING AND PROOFREADING

<u>Revising</u>

Revising your essay definitely improves the quality of your work. You want to submit your best work to the teacher, so revising is necessary to identify any problems within the essay; problems with clarity, coherence, support, specificity, logic, organization, style and tone, but not grammar and punctuation problems (called proofreading). Examining and revising your rough draft will benefit the work and perhaps your grade.

EXERCISE 1.11

Examine the paragraphs below. Revise the work (in your area) to improve paragraph coherence, logic, and the topic sentence. Rearrange the sentences for clarity and organization. Eliminate sentences that are not appropriate.

Allied Health

Between 1 and 3 months of age, infants begin to synthesize their own immunoglobulins.(1) Infections are a major cause of death in newborns, who have immature immune systems and are protected for only the first 2 or 3 months by immunoglobulins passively received from the mother.(2) Immunizations against diphtheria, tetanus, and pertussis are usually started at 2 months, when the infant's immune system can respond.(3) That's a really great thing to do for the child.(4) Whether a microorganism causes an infection depends on a number of factors already mentioned.(5) Age influences the risk of infection.(6) One of the most important factors is host susceptibility, which is affected by age, heredity, level of stress, nutritional status, current medical therapy, and preexisting disease processes.(7) In other words, everything contributes to a baby's problems.(8) Newborns and older adults have reduced defenses against infection.(9)

AutoCAD

On the drafting board, all drawings are committed to paper from the start.(1) The AutoCAD plotting system takes full advantage of the powers of a CAD system, allowing us to ignore scale and other drawing paper issues entirely, if we wish, until it is time to plot.(2) Up to now, we have plotted everything directly from model space.(3) However, when your focus shifts from modeling issues to presentation issues, paper space layouts have much more to offer.(4) When draftspeople first begin using CAD systems, they still tend to think in terms of the final hard copy their plotter will produce even as they are creating lines on the screen.(5) Plotting from model spaces has its uses, particularly in the early stages of a design process.(6) The separation of model space and paper space in AutoCAD allows you to focus entirely on modeling and real-world dimensions when you are drawing, and then shifts your focus to paper output issues when you plot.(7) People doing manual drafting are inevitably conscious of scale, paper size, and rotation from start to finish.(8) Drafting is truly an art.(9)

Automotive Technology

Whenever the engine rotates faster than the starter pinion, the balls or rollers are forced out of the narrow tapered notch, allowing the pinion gear to turn freely.(1) This clutch is called an overrunning clutch, and it protects the starter motor from damage if the ignition switch is held in the start position after the engine starts.(2) Engines are complicated things.(3) All starter drive mechanisms use a type of one-way clutch that allows the starter to rotate the engine, but that turns freely if the engine speed is greater than the starter motor speed.(4) This taper forces the balls or rollers tightly into the notch when rotation is in the direction necessary to start the engine.(5)

The overrunning clutch, which is built in as part of the starter drive unit, uses steel balls or rollers installed in tapered notches.(6)

Criminal Justice

Psychotic people have also been classified as schizophrenic or paranoid schizophrenic.(1) Paranoia is a treatable mental disorder.(2) The classic psychotic thinks he or she is Napoleon or sees spiders covering what others perceive as a bare wall.(3) Psychosis can be dangerous.(4) Another form of mental disorder is called psychosis.(5) Psychoses may either be organic (that is, caused by physical damage to, or abnormalities in, the brain) or functional (that is, with no known physical cause).(6) Schizophrenics are said to be characterized by disordered or disjointed thinking.(7) Psychotic people, according to psychiatric definitions, are out of touch with reality in some fundamental way.(8) They may suffer from hallucinations, delusions, or other breaks with reality.(9)

Electronics

We have all seen a permanent magnet pick up paper clips, nails, or iron filings.(1) When removed from the magnetic field, the object tends to lose its magnetism.(2) These domains can be viewed as very small bar magnets with north and south poles.(3) Magnets are very powerful.(4) Ferromagnetic materials such as iron, nickel, and cobalt become magnetized when placed in the magnetic field of a magnet.(5) In these cases, the object becomes magnetized (that is, it actually becomes a magnet itself) under the influence of the permanent magnetic field and becomes attracted to the magnet.(6) Thus, the object itself effectively becomes a magnet.(7) Ferromagnetic materials have minute magnetic domains created within their atomic structure by the orbital motion and spin of electrons.(8) When the material is not exposed to an external magnetic field, the magnetic domains are randomly oriented.(9) When the material is placed in a magnetic field, the domains align themselves.(10)

Information Technology

In contrast to the processing of individual transactions, these applications help managers oversee and make decisions about company or department operations.(1) Transaction processing uses a combination of information technology and manual procedures to process data and information and to manage transactions.(2) These are very complicated activities.(3) In today's world, however, companies often refer to business management applications, called information systems or management information systems.(4) Programs created to manage business activities made up the bulk of the software industry prior to the PC boom in the late 1970s and early 1980s.(5) For years, businesses have used this system to process transaction data for payroll management, production management, personnel records management, inventory control, and accounting procedures.(6) Obviously, computer transactions are extremely important in business.(7) Even today, transaction processing applications account for huge expenditures of business funds in both large and small organizations.(8)

Paralegal

They often address certain aspects of the cause of action.(1) If it is unclear whether the substantive or procedural issues are to be examined, the paralegal should check with the person requesting the briefs.(2) It is always a good idea to check with the appropriate attorney.(3) One example is a question such as, "Did the defendant answer the plaintiff's complaint within the allotted twenty-day time period if the answer was mailed and postmarked within that period?"(4) If an attorney is asking the paralegal to brief a number of cases dealing with the elements of assault, the attorney is clearly looking for the substantive issues in the cases.(5) Make certain you are aware of what the attorney is looking for.(6) Other questions are known as substantive issues because they deal with the actual substance of legal rights.(7) In an assault case, an example of a substantive issue might be, "Can an assault be committed against another without actual physical contact?"(8) Procedural issues are so labeled because they deal only with procedure and the manner in which a case is handled by the judicial system.(9)

_____

_____

_____

_____

_____

_____

_____

_____

_____

_____

_____

_____

_____

<u>Proofreading</u>

Proofreading is an essential part of submitting quality work. You want to submit as professional a paper as is possible; therefore, you need to check for spelling, punctuation, and grammar problems. (While SpellCheck and GrammarCheck may be helpful, they are not substitutes for knowledge and judgment.)

❧ *EXERCISE 1.12* ❧

Examine the paragraphs below and correct the errors as you find them.

A. In an ideel world people will do waht they sposed to but people are people despite good intents things don't always work out the way we'de like them to. Even though your freinds and family may be aware of you're need to study for a test or write a paper they may still ask you to accompanie them someware—sometimes it it is necessarie to say no to people!!!!!!!!!! Sometimes saying NO!!$)**^#??//! Is the only way you can compleate college assignmts saying no need not be a bad or negative word but merly a way to assurt you're need to do the work you need too do to complete your long range goal. Which you need to do if you want to graduate. If you need to say "no" say it in in a pozitive and reassureing way remind family and freinds that school takes procedence over what they might want from you. For their benefit. you need to study don't you so that you can past the test so that you can past the class so the you can get the degree so that you can get the job you want so that you can improve the qualitie of your life and theirs.

B. Cririal thinking is a skill biased in logic and reason. Which when applied to any and all situations, condetions, and issue, can impovre the qualitie of you're personal and profesional live? Critical thinking can aid in resolution-conflicts, probleme solving communicating more effectivly managing your tyme, taking tests, and even improving you're relashunships. Which we could all use. Unfortunately because, many of us lack the skills of good critical thinking, were relegated to responding to most situatens and people in purely emotionl ways? if however, you learn touse the skills of criticla thinking you can become more sucessful students friends employees.

Part II
Writing Styles

Chapter 2
Narration

Narrative Writing

TIPS

Definition

Use the narrative style to express emotion and/or to tell a story. Description, dialogue, and the first perspectives are common features of narrative writing. The narrative writing style usually tells a story in chronological order.

Career Uses

In the workplace, narrative writing describes incidents that may require further action, such as an accident or disciplinary matter. Most supervisors have to write narratives describing a situation from memory using facts with supporting details. These reports provide important information to evaluate the need for possible further action. For example: *"Last night between 7:10-7:20pm, I heard a crash in the hallway followed by the sound of running. I quickly alerted the other officer on duty and chased after the inmate."*

Principles of Narrative Writing

How do you know when to use narrative writing? Look for these types of questions or prompts:

- *Describe your experience . . .*

- *Tell about . . .*

- *Relate what happened . . .*

- *Write a story about. . .*

- *What do you do to. . .*

When you see one of these phrases, respond using narrative style. Narrative writing answers the questions of **who, when,** and **where**. Be sure to include answers to these questions in your writing to help organize your information and to report facts. The chain of events, emotions, or ideas occurs in a logical order. Often, connecting words tie the events of the passage together, such as *then, now, first, second, later,* and *lastly.* (Stating the information in first person using active verbs eliminates passive descriptions.)

Avoid these Common Mistakes

Here are some of the common mistakes made by writers when using narrative style. Read the following two versions of each type of common mistake noting the difference between the examples.

- *Avoid writing long character-narrated introductions rather than using immediate action:* **He stood five feet tall almost reaching the top of the counter, hair draped just over his eyes and a sneer that covered the whole of his face. He seemed to be considering his next move; maybe he will move towards the door to avoid seeing her.**

- *Instead use action words to provide movement and interest:* Quickly, he darted from the counter to the door in an effort to avoid her. A blur of hair and sneer, he exploded onto the street, his five foot frame carrying him away from the building at blinding speed.

- *Show rather than tell the reader about something that is beautiful or ugly:* I think that the house is a drab shade of grey with dark shutters. There are cracks in the sides of the doors where the paint has worn away.

- *Describe conditions of items and people using vivid language that invites the reader to feel as if he/she is actually experiencing the narrative.* Approaching the house on foot was no easy task, the underbrush warned intruders, such as myself, to stay away. Before reaching the front of the house, there was a fantastic creak followed by a crash. A cracked door swung, as in pain, from its hinges. Closer, the dark shutters clanked against the house throwing chips of grey paint to the ground.

- *Do not say the same thing in many different ways—once is enough.* I heard the sound from the backyard; it startled me. The sound came from the backyard and was startling.

- *Write your original idea and add details.* A sudden sound from the backyard startled me, sending me across the kitchen to see the source. Shaking, I beamed a light onto the patio, uncertain of what I might find.

EXERCISES

Rewrite each sentence in narrative style. Change or add as few words as possible. Identify the main subject in the sentence and then construct a new sentence using active verbs with some description. For example,

> **Clinical internships are required for surgical technology students.**
> **"I am excited about my clinical internship assignment to St. John's Hospital next semester: it is the best hospital in our area."**

Allied Health

1. Today, the majority of patients had the flu.

   _____

2. There are so many different fields of medicine; choosing a specialty is challenging.

   _____

3. Use special care to calm a nervous patient before giving an injection.

   _____

4. Dental assistants practice universal procedures to protect themselves from disease, though some patients vehemently complain.

   _____

   _____

5. To advance his career, he decided to return to school to earn his registered nursing license.

   _____

   _____

6. Working in a doctor's office can be stressful, at times.

   _____

7. Shauna decided to study medical billing and coding so that she can work from home.

   _____

8. While RJ was taking a medical history with a patient, he discovered that the patient is allergic to sulfa drugs.

   _____

   _____

9. Once in school, Carlos decided to switch majors from medical assisting to pharmacy technology.

_____

_____

10. Dental assistants learn to position film in patients' mouths so that they show various angles.

_____

_____

AutoCAD

1. The student asked his instructor to explain, again, the difference between polar and orthographic tracking.

_____

_____

2. When he completes his degree, John will work for a major animation studio.

_____

3. Marc discovered problems with the structural design for the addition planned for the house.

_____

_____

4. Learning to use the gradient fill tools properly takes a lot of experimentation with color and shading.

_____

_____

5. Even though the characters were finished, none of the backgrounds fit with the storyboard.

_____

_____

6. She needed to decide whether to take landscaping or jewelry design classes next semester.

_____

7. Unfortunately, the original dimensions for the building have to be revised, according to the client.

_____

_____

8. Aeronautical engineers create aircraft using three-dimensional imaging.

_____

9. The students enjoyed their Fundamentals of AutoCAD class.

_____

10. She met with the architects yesterday; they want her to design a second floor for the house.

_____

_____

Automotive Technology

1. The mechanic had always dreamed of working on diesel engines.

_____

2. An angry woman is pacing in the waiting room; she insists that her car was not fixed properly.

_____

_____

3. Though no one else heard the sound, James is certain that a belt is loose.

_____

4. Sally purchased a new set of flare nut wrenches yesterday.

_____

5. The battery died overnight and Mr. Sanchez was going to be late for work.

_____

6. After months of work, the proud mechanic started the engine of her 1964 Mustang.

_____

7. With the engine steaming, Mr. Jones drove his car onto the median so that he could call for assistance.

_____

_____

8. Every time that Kerri fills the windshield wiper reservoir, it leaks onto the driveway.

_____

9. It takes experience and patience to properly diagnose engine problems.

_____

10. For the third time this month, Mr. Jones had a flat tire.

_____

Criminal Justice

1. The police officer arrested three men and charged them with possession of cocaine.

   _____

2. It can be frustrating to interview an uncooperative suspect.

   _____

3. After learning of his positive drug screen, the probationer begged for another chance.

   _____

4. Collecting evidence, the investigator found a bullet buried in the wall behind the chair.

   _____

5. During the game, officers surrounded the players as they moved from the locker room to the stadium.

   _____

   _____

6. Each time the President visited the city, the agent knew that he would work on the security detail.

   _____

   _____

7. To be promoted to detective, the officer must pass a test and interview with the review board.

   _____

   _____

8. Most new officers work the overnight shift for four days of the week.

   _____

9. Juveniles who serve their sentences in boot camps report higher non-arrest rates than those who serve sentences in detention centers.

   _____

   _____

10. Mrs. Jones called the county Code Violations office to report an abandoned car in her neighborhood.

   _____

   _____

Electronics

1. Max completed the schematic of the batteries to send to the designer.

   _____

2. For homework, the instructor told the students to memorize the SI units and symbols for the exam at the end of the week.

    _____

    _____

3. She applied Kirchhoff's voltage law to determine the number of voltage drops.

    _____

4. During the storm, the circuits overloaded causing power outages in residences across town.

    _____

    _____

5. Your stereo system is to be wired to an Audio Signal Generator.

    _____

6. Before beginning work on the wiring, the electrician disconnected the transistor.

    _____

7. After graduation, she wants to use her electrical knowledge to write technical manuals.

    _____

8. He had to connect his first polarized capacitor; he remembers that it could explode if connected backwards.

    _____

    _____

9. Learning to troubleshoot wiring problems comes with experience.

    _____

10. Ely ordered a new oscilloscope because the old one gives irregular readings.

    _____

Information Technology

1. Searching for a solution for slow sales, the business partners decide to hire a web designer to create an e-commerce site.

    _____

    _____

2. Marta feels nervous about the computer training in the morning; she has not worked with a computer for very long.

    _____

    _____

3. Frustrated with the continuous failure of the server, Gene decides to reroute half of the computers to a second server in an effort to improve system function.

_____

_____

4. The phones are flooded with excited questions about the new operating system that is to be released next week.

_____

_____

5. His computer, attacked by a malicious computer virus, needs reformatting.

_____

6. Late one night, Jack tapped into the main database of his company to check his personnel file, despite his worries of being caught.

_____

_____

7. Lee wants to upgrade her CPU so that she can work with three programs simultaneously; she cannot do this with her current processor.

_____

_____

8. The recruiter insists that the job requires a candidate with C++ certification and knowledge of Java-script programming.

_____

_____

9. She explained to her mother that she could pay her bills online without fear of security issues.

_____

_____

10. Knowing that he had to update his medical office, Dr. Medeiros called the programmer to arrange for installation of computers.

_____

_____

Paralegal Studies

1. To earn an Associate's degree in paralegal studies, it will take two years of full-time study.

_____

_____

2. Paralegal assistants must avoid situations that present a conflict of interest; it is not ethical.

_____

_____

3. Her first job in the legal field is to complete foreclosure documentation for a real estate firm.

_____

_____

4. Ben cannot decide whether he should take legal research or constitutional law classes next.

_____

_____

5. You must disclose your position as a legal assistant to clients before beginning work for them.

_____

_____

6. He struggled to pass his tort class; he did not find time to study.

_____

7. While conducting research for the case, Maria noticed that the headnote contained a lead.

_____

8. Three paralegal assistants and a legal secretary will be hired to work for the new partner.

_____

9. One of the functions of a paralegal assistant is to conduct preliminary research for a case.

_____

10. The couple met with the legal assistant to complete their divorce papers in preparation for the hearing.

_____

_____

Arrange these sentences into a paragraph and write your new paragraph in the space below. Find the topic sentence first, and then create a story using the rest of the sentences in logical order.

Allied Health

1. "Mr. Brody, you are scheduled for surgery in the morning; you cannot eat pizza."

2. Mr. Brody, in room 3A, has spent the past three hours insisting that he needs a pizza.

3. Despite my protestations, he continued these complaints.

4. It was later in the afternoon that I finally understood his request when his grandson visited and asked for his Tuesday pizza.

5. I am losing my patience with him.

6. "Nurse, grant me this one wish, please," he pleaded.

_____

_____

_____

_____

AutoCAD

1. He was right; I wish that we had listened to him.

2. Ambient? Distant? We tried every conceivable combination of lighting without success.

3. Frantically, John and I worked late into the night, desperate to complete our project before morning.

4. As the colored light flooded the studio, we started laughing; we found the perfect lighting for our image.

5. Our instructor warned us that rendering the images would take hours of experimentation.

6. Tired and frustrated, John walked to the window and raised the shade to reveal the sunrise.

_____

_____

_____

_____

Automotive Technology

1. "Do you think that I want the whole world to look at me, I cannot control this," I seethed.

2. At last, we arrived at the service station; my mechanic rushed out and implored me to stop leaning on the horn.

3. My friend glared at me while sinking down in his seat as we passed other cars.

4. "This is just embarrassing," my friend sighed.

5. As my friend jumped into the car, he questioned, "Why are you honking your horn when there is no other car in sight?"

6. Irritated by the cacophony and looks that I drew from other motorists, I decided to drive to the service station.

_____

_____

_____

_____

Criminal Justice

1. Concerned that he had driven to the office alone, I asked if he had been drinking.

2. Again, he stated that he was not going to cooperate and that he was leaving.

3. The probationer, smelling of alcohol, reported to my office at 16:00.

4. He sullenly replied that he was not going to answer any of my questions because he was only there to pay his probation fees.

5. I felt that due to his continued elusiveness and failure to admit to his need for help, I had to report him as being in violation of his probation.

6. I asked him again if he had been drinking, with the intention of calling his substance abuse counselor so that they could discuss the relapse.

_____

_____

_____

_____

Electronics

1. To prepare, I reviewed my notes about wiring the opener to the house current; this was to be an easy job.

2. My first job as an independent contractor was not as successful as I would have liked.

3. When she pushed the remote button, sparks flew from inside the garage; worse, the garage door next door opened!

4. Mrs. Garcia called to hire me to install her garage door opener.

5. After hours of struggling to get the connections to work, I called Mrs. Garcia to test her new garage door opener.

6. Finally, I arrived to begin work; Mrs. Garcia gave me the kit and left me to work.

_____

_____

_____

_____

Information Technology

1. So, I poured some coffee and waited for the engineer from the first floor to appear.

2. As I opened my mouth to respond, a member of the billing staff walked in complaining of the same problem.

3. Before I had the opportunity to check my email, Ms. Blackwell called to tell me that the morning's first appointment had arrived.

4. I entered my office and turned on my computer, like every morning.

5. Hands in the air, I assured both that the problem would be solved by the end of the day.

6. It was only a moment before he stormed through the door shouting that their database was wrong; he could only access the one from the billing department.

_____

_____

_____

_____

Paralegal Studies

1. As I approached the car, I heard, from behind, the pounding of footsteps on the pavement.

2. So, I left the building and trudged to my car, briefcase heavy in hand.

3. Thankfully, I recognized the man as a client of our law office.

4. "I just called your office. Thank you so much for helping me with my divorce settlement. Without your expertise, I would not have been able to get through this."

5. I turned sharply with my heart racing as the person neared.

6. The phone rang as my hand reached for the light switch, reluctant to stay any longer; I chose to ignore the call.

_____

_____

_____

_____

❧ EXERCISE 2.3 ❧

The next writing sample is missing the topic sentence. Read the paragraph to decide what information is the most important, then write a sentence as an introduction to the material.

Allied Health

_____. (topic sentence)
Later that evening, watching the ambulance pull away, George remembered leaving his glasses in the back while transporting the patient. Panicked, he called dispatch to contact the driver. Unfortunately, the medics did not respond as they had already answered a call across town. Frustrated, George reported back to his floor to continue his shift.

AutoCAD

_____. (topic sentence)
He was pleasant on the phone, however, it did not sound as if they are willing to train any interns now. If I can't find a company willing to train me for next semester, I will not be able to graduate. I do not need to take any other classes for my degree. "Do you know of any other jewelry design company in town?"

Automotive Technology

_____. (topic sentence)

"No sir, the car is in good condition," Matt insisted. He smiled as he dreamed of his new car. The salesman nodded, knowingly as he leaned against Matt's car. As he did, the car began to roll forward. Matt sighed; he neglected to mention the defective emergency brake.

Criminal Justice

_____. (topic sentence)

Then, without any hesitation, he drove straight through the light. I honked to get him to slow down; however, he seemed not to notice. Before I knew it, he had hit not only the car in front of him, but also, the one to his left. It was then that I called for the ambulance and police.

Electronics

_____. (topic sentence)

And this was only my first day of my apprenticeship. You would not believe the size of this studio; it is one of the largest radio studios in the city. All of the sound booths need to have the equipment replaced—this job will take us most of the summer to finish. I do not mind though; in just one day, I have learned so much. I cannot wait to go back tomorrow!

Information Technology

_____. (topic sentence)

Then, I plugged the phone line into the back of the computer and turned it on. Excited to search the Internet, I started my browser. After waiting for minutes for the program to connect, I realized that something was still not working properly. On my hands and knees, I checked the back of the computer for loose connections. Still, I saw nothing amiss. As I was doing this, my phone rang and I suddenly realized what I had forgotten!

Paralegal Studies

_____. (topic sentence)

The next thing I knew, I was snoring with my face in the casebook. I honestly do not know how long I was asleep before Max found me. Now, if he had just roused me, it would not have been so bad; there was still time to complete the work. I realize that he did not know that I was to deliver the research to Mr. Morgan by 3:00 P.M. Still, I wish that he would have shaken me or something; now I am in trouble.

EXERCISE 2.4

In this exercise, the last sentence is missing. Write one that logically concludes the idea.

Allied Health

I remember the difficulty of finding my first job in a hospital. First, I applied to County General Hospital; they offered me a position working as an itinerant medical assistant. The pay is tempting; however, I need to work steady hours. Now, City Central Hospital offered less money, but steady shifts. Both implied that I could work extra shifts as desired. _____ _____. (concluding sentence)

AutoCAD

While working on the project, I discovered that I could change the background colors, shading, and dimensions using the fill tools. In fact, I had so much fun exploring, that I decided to alter my drawings so that they are set against dramatic settings. I showed the final project to my instructor, proud of my work. _____ _____. (concluding sentence)

Automotive Technology

"You will not believe the estimates that I heard for painting my car," Susan told her friend. "The man at the first shop wants $400 because the car is a custom color. The next estimate was much cheaper, $250; however, they are not able to match the car's original color. Next, I called your cousin, like you suggested. He is too busy. _____ _____." (concluding sentence)

Criminal Justice

Someone stole my station wagon while I was in Michigan visiting my parents. I arrived home from my vacation late last night. I took a cab home from the airport. Because I was so tired, I did not notice that anything was wrong. It was not until this morning when I entered my garage that I discovered the broken windows. _____ _____. (concluding sentence)

Electronics

In class, we learned about the importance of grounding currents before beginning work with voltages. I admit that I am a little worried about electrocution due to a mistake. Then again, the process of grounding is not complicated and I did take notes. Still, I know how to fix basic electrical problems while following safety precautions. _____ _____. (concluding sentence)

Information Technology

I cannot believe that I am lost! In fifteen minutes, I am to interview for my first job as an information specialist. How different this feels from yesterday when, I practically ran across the stage exuberant to accept my degree. Ironic that I would take a wrong turn with all of the information that I am able to access—wish that I'd thought to print a map from the web. Hmm that's right; I can access the Internet from my phone. _____

_____. (concluding sentence)

Paralegal Studies

Today, I began working for Brown & Richter, you know, the big law firm on the other side of town. It was a difficult first day, as first days go, that is. Just as I settled into my chair and started to read my first research case, an old client from my last firm passed through the office. Distracted, I opened the folder and began to read. It took a few minutes for me to realize that I was reading information about my old client, which is a clear ethics violation. _____

_____. (concluding sentence)

❧ EXERCISE 2.5 ❧

Now that you have practiced writing topic and concluding sentences, write both for the next exercise. To do this, add necessary information to introduce and to close the paragraph.

Allied Health

_____. And then, we rushed to the woman who was prone on the pavement. Just as we learned in class, we checked her airway, breathing, and pulse. With no signs of heart beat or breath, we started to administer CPR as we learned in class. The minutes seemed closer to hours when the paramedics arrived to relieve us.

_____.

AutoCAD

_____.

And then, I bought a coffeemaker, even though I do not drink coffee. What a creative project this is; it will be fun to design a new coffee pot. This allows me to use my solid modeling skills.

_____.

Automotive Technology

_____.

I know that we cleaned the terminals and wires. We tested and changed the battery. Honestly, there must be something else that we are missing. The car is still experiencing intermittent power surges. _____.

Criminal Justice

_____.

So, I can take you and the children to a shelter for the evening. You will be safe there until we are able to find your boyfriend. The only other option that I can offer is to check on you in the morning if you choose to stay here. _____

_____.

Electronics

_____.

So, after speaking with the woman at the Career Center, I am excited about my prospects as an air condition technician. According to her, there is an excellent chance of my finding a job following the completion of my apprenticeship. I scheduled another appointment with her so that she can help me write my resume. _____

_____.

Information Technology

_____.

I then carried my coffee and laptop to the only available table. Settling into my seat, I started my laptop and checked for an Internet signal. When I did not see one, I realized that I would have to wait for another table to open: one that is in the hotspot. I wondered how I would know which areas could capture the signal. _____

_____.

Paralegal Studies

_____.

She tried again, to explain to the caller that she could not help him save his house. Her job is to file paperwork for the last step before foreclosure. No matter what she said, the man continued to yell. When he finished, she calmly asked if he had any questions. _____

_____.

The challenge in writing a narrative is to create a clear topic sentence, one that invites the interest and emotion of the reader. Before writing, try telling your story aloud. Remember to include who, when, and where in your storyline. Write a paragraph in the space below. Once finished, ask someone to read it to you so that you can hear the story. While listening to the story, try to create pictures of the events in your head. This will help you to create a sense of beginning and ending to your paragraphs.

Topic: Tell about a time in your life when you felt motivated to complete a project. What motivated you and how did you use that motivation?

_____

_____

_____

_____

_____

_____

_____

Descriptive Writing

TIPS

Definition

Descriptive writing creates pictures of scenes, portrays characters, or relates an experience using the five senses. Writers also employ this style to describe an exact location of an object. To properly illustrate a location, writers use words to describe placement. In addition, writers create interest in a description through the use of comparisons of two unlike items. For example, one might compare a car to a beast to describe the similarities and/or differences.

Career Uses

Traditionally, descriptive writing recreates a scene and/or experience for incident reports, case/medical notes, and diagnostic reports. The writer uses specific detail to help the reader understand the sequence of events or description of a situation. Descriptive writing is an essential skill for anyone who writes notes for others to follow. For example, a manager of an automotive repair shop writes work orders according to information reported by the customer. If the information is not complete, then the mechanic will waste time diagnosing the problem. For example: *According to the customer, every time the car slows to stop, there is a loud whining sound followed by a thud. Then, the engine stalls and both the engine and oil lights flash. Check the car's computer first, and then check all belts. Call customer with a repair estimate after completing diagnosis.*

Principles of Descriptive Writing

How do you know when to use descriptive writing? Look for these types of questions or prompts:

- *Describe a time in your life when . . .*

- *Describe the location of . . .*

- *Describe your feeling when. . . .*

- *Tell of an important person in your life . . .*

- *Give your impression of . . .*

When asked to write a description or impression of something, use the descriptive writing style. Descriptive writing illustrates events chronologically in exacting detail using adjectives and adverbs. The descriptive essay relies on concrete, sensory detail to communicate the information. The author of a descriptive essay must carefully select details to support the main point. To effectively write a description, choose an outstanding characteristic of the event or person. For example, if writing about a football game, choose one perspective in terms of excitement or boredom, not both. Lastly, descriptive writing is strongest when told in chronological order.

Avoid these Common Mistakes

Here are some of the common mistakes made by writers when using descriptive style:

- *Avoid overloading the description with adjectives and adverbs when using this style. Add only one or two adjectives or adverbs to create an impression; using more will confuse the description. Choose words that are essential to the overall story rather than ones that do not add any important information.* For example, instead of writing about the short, loud man who drove a broken-down car into the shop, write about the car that pulled into the garage blowing smoke from the exhaust. The information about the man is not essential to the description of the car's problem. In the second example, the writer describes the car's problem.

- *Do not attempt to describe events without giving a logical chronology.* For example, instead of writing that the client was arraigned, arrested, and charged with aggravated assault is confusing. Organize the facts according to the order in which they occurred.

- *Do not focus on more than one point of view per description.* Avoid changing the perspective of the description; to do so is to confuse the reader as to the origin of the facts.

EXERCISES

⟨ EXERCISE 2.7 ⟩

Rewrite each sentence using descriptive style. Change or add as few words as possible. Identify the main subject in the sentence and then construct a new sentence using active verbs with some description. For example:

Original Sentence: **The patient demanded an emergency appointment because of a severe toothache.**

Rewritten Sentence: **Standing at the receptionist's desk, the woman, holding her jaw in excruciating pain, demanded an emergency appointment to have her tooth examined.**

Allied Health

1. Quietly, the nurse entered the room to wake the patient to administer his medications.

2. The emergency room is filled with people who are ill; there are three more ambulances parked in front holding more patients.

3. The pharmacy technologist carefully prepared Mr. Garcia's pills.

4. Following the page, the medical assistant reported to the lab to offer help with the patient.

5. Due to the urgency of the operation, the surgical technologist did not have enough time to complete preparations in the operating room before the surgeon arrived.

6. The medical assistant struggled to record the medical history of a deaf patient.

7. Phyllis practiced drawing blood from other classmates in preparation for her phlebotomy exam.

8. Nervously, the young man rushed to the admissions desk; his wife is ready to give birth.

9. The patient accidentally knocked the tray of sterilized dental instruments on the floor.

10. In the emergency room, a woman shouts for assistance with her child.

AutoCAD

1. All agreed that the text box needs reformatting because it interferes with the images.

2. The directions say to create a 3D image of a garage.

3. Jason wants to add video to the animation; he is unsure how to do this.

4. Troubled by the fuzzy edges, she tried to reconfigure the left side of the picture.

5. Using the measurements provided by the drawing, the carpenter built the deck.

6. To practice rendering, Marie worked in the animation lab.

7. The students added surface generation to their projects.

8. According to the directions, the circumference of the circle is used to set the coordinates for the equilateral triangle.

9. Frustrated, Anne tried to draw on the Xref layer; the program does not allow this.

10. Knowing that the architect needed the dimensions changed, the designer tried to balance the available space with the new additions.

Automotive Technology

1. Learning to diagnose engine problems requires a mechanic to use sight and hearing.

2. The left, passenger side tire is flat from a nail puncture.

3. Noticing the dirt in the air filter, the technician removed it to show the customer.

4. The dealer recommends that drivers living in cold weather climates purchase vehicles with all-wheel drive.

5. To fix the timing belt, the mechanic removed the engine from the car.

6. When the oil light stays on, the driver should check the fluid level immediately.

7. Before authorizing work done to his car, he requires an estimate of all needed repairs.

8. She always wanted to rebuild foreign cars.

9. Due to increased business, the owner decided to extend service hours at the garage.

10. After replacing the transmission, the mechanic realized that the input shaft was cracked.

Criminal Justice

1. Due to the rise in crimes, undercover officers are stationed along Market Street to investigate the increased drug trafficking in the area.

2. Last night, two officers arrested the car thief outside of the market.

3. The new police cruisers contain mobile computers.

4. To learn about the effects of drug addiction, students visited a residential drug treatment facility.

5. The animal control officer arrived at the scene in time to see the raccoon escape into the woods.

6. Children gathered at the field to watch the K9 unit demonstration during field day.

7. The school resource officer spoke to the students during a school assembly; he taught them about the dangers of drug use.

8. From the window in his office, the probation officer watched a drug deal in the parking lot.

9. To allay the fear of the woman, the officers checked the unlocked house before she entered.

10. The crowd at the college football game became unruly when the home team won.

Electronics

1. The electrician suggested that he buy a plate for the outlet to cover the connections.

2. Uncoiled wires indicated an open circuit; the washing machine did not work because of it.

3. During class, the students shorted their battery as they accidentally crossed polarized wires.

4. The battery lost its charge each time Stephen tried to connect it to the boat.

5. To fix the leaky capacitor, Angel tested the discharge values.

6. He checked the voltage-divider board to see how to modify it to direct four voltage levels.

7. To earn extra money, he agreed to wire the new sound board for the school.

8. Janet studied the resistor color codes for her exam on Monday.

9. Students practiced diagnosing symptoms of specific component failures.

10. She connected the last wire on the radio; it crackled as it received the signal.

Information Technology

1. After feeling heat from the underside of her laptop, she decided to turn off the power.

2. When lightening struck the building, the server's connection overloaded.

3. Frustrated with the lack of processing speed, Jorge ran the worm detection program.

4. IT students, in partnership with electronics students, built a robotic arm for the fair.

5. The customer wants to add another USB port to her laptop.

6. During his online class, the electronic bulletin board crashed; he lost all of his class postings.

7. There is a loud churning sound coming from the hard drive.

8. The company sent the wrong cable for the connection.

9. William will work as an analyst for the university upon graduating.

10. E-commerce businesses need to hire programmers for around-the-clock system monitoring.

Paralegal Studies

1. In order to prepare for trial, the legal assistant wrote three subpoenas.

2. Running across town to deliver a brief, the paralegal worried that he would be too late.

3. The client requested a consultation regarding filing divorce papers.

4. Due to the complicated nature of the personal injury case, the legal assistant conducted most of the witness interviews.

5. The lawyer asked the paralegal to take notes during the deposition so that future research can be conducted for the case.

6. To increase her marketability, she applied for a part-time paralegal position in the hospital.

7. The paralegal spent the night in the legal library conducting research for a murder trial.

8. Upon graduating from college, the paralegals worked as consultants for companies that needed specialized legal services.

9. Preparing a codicil to his client's will, the legal assistant discovered that he is named as a recipient of a portion of the estate.

10. Excited about handling her first closing, the paralegal thanked her supervisor for her guidance.

❖ *EXERCISE 2.8* ❖

Arrange these sentences into a paragraph and write the new paragraph in the space below. Find the topic sentence first, and then create a story using the rest of the sentences in logical order.

Allied Health

1. "Your next patient is here," announced the receptionist as I prepared my instruments.

2. In the gentlest voice I could muster, I assured him that he would not be hurt and that the dentist and I would be careful.

3. Palpable fear filled the room as I approached; I slowly offered my outstretched hand to him.

4. I entered the waiting room to see a young boy clinging to his mother, arms clenched around her neck.

5. Watching my approach, he squeaked almost too quiet to hear, "Please, please don't hurt me."

6. In response, his pleading eyes matched the terrified pitch in his voice, "I hate the dentist. I hate to get my teeth cleaned. Please Mommy!"

_____

_____

_____

_____

_____

AutoCAD

1. And finally, the movie ended to thunderous applause.

2. The room darkened and as my eyes focused on the screen, my excitement rose with each note of the soundtrack.

3. This evening my partner and I stood mesmerized by the big screen; before us was our first animated film in glorious, colored action.

4. With these thoughts running in my head, my partner turned to me grinning widely, possibly sharing my memories.

5. A year ago, it was impossible to envision this finished project; we struggled to render our animations, to refine their movements.

6. As our creation played on screen, I glanced at my partner remembering our year of continuous, painstaking work.

_____

_____

_____

_____

_____

Automotive Technology

1. Even with smoke blowing from the tailpipe, the mechanic was still uncertain of the exact origin of the problem.

2. More smoke arose from the back of the car; puzzled by the problem, the mechanic parked the car.

3. Suspecting a coolant leak, he checked the transmission reservoir only to find it empty.

4. As the engine cooled, the mechanic noticed a pungent odor coming from the passenger side of the car.

5. To diagnose the car's problem, the mechanic decided to drive it around the block.

6. Happy to discover the problem, the mechanic returned to the garage to fix the coolant leak.

_____

_____

_____

_____

_____

_____

Criminal Justice

1. As I passed each of them, their eyes following me, I noted their expressions: hollow and angry, even defeated.

2. Despite this dark feeling, I remembered my excitement.

3. It took several moments for my eyes to adjust to the diminished lights of each successive corridor.

4. Once I focused my eyes, I wondered at the starkness, the ugliness, the emptiness mirrored in the faces of the prisoners.

5. "Clank-clank-clank," one by one the heavy steel doors echoed behind me closing immediately as I passed through the front door into the dark hallway.

6. This is my first day as their guard.

_____

_____

_____

_____

_____

_____

Electronics

1. Frustrated, she pulled out the heater coil and fit it back into the slot.

2. She placed the pot on the burner to heat the water and left it to heat.

3. Within minutes, the water boiled over the side of the pot.

4. Feeling exhausted after working a double shift, Anita turned on her stove to start dinner.

5. Once again, she switched on the power for the burner and placed the pot on it.

6. After waiting for ages, Anita waved her hand over the burner to check for heat; there was none.

_____

_____

_____

_____

_____

_____

Information Technology

1. If all connections are correct, then the printer will print a test document.

2. First, place the hard drive in its permanent location.

3. Check the back of both for diagrams illustrating the proper connection port.

4. Once both the hard drive and monitor are situated, connect the cable.

5. Next, decide on a location for the monitor; be sure to check the length of the cable connection between the computer and the monitor.

6. Test the connection by turning on the computer and monitor; if both work, attach the printer cable to the backs of the printer and computer.

_____

_____

_____

_____

_____

_____

Paralegal Studies

1. In response to the verdict, the plaintiff grabbed hold of his lawyer's hand and excitedly pumped it.

2. He reassured the defendant that justice would still prevail.

3. The courtroom, charged with anticipation, erupted with the reading of the verdict.

4. Once the celebrating ceased and all sat, the judge announced the date for the sentencing hearing.

5. Following the judge's announcement of sentencing, the defendant's lawyer calmly explained the appeal process.

6. Watching this, the defendant sat daring not to move as the plaintiff celebrated.

_____

_____

_____

_____

_____

_____

❧ *EXERCISE 2.9* ❧

The next writing sample is missing the topic sentence. Read the paragraph to decide what information is the most important, and then write an introduction to the material.

Allied Health

_____. (topic sentence)
Exhausted, the surgical technologist sank into her chair to nap. Within moments, a loud crash interrupted her sleep. She sprang up to see a young child before her. The child smiled as he extended his hand pointing towards an upturned cart. Without speaking, he pointed towards the cart and then to himself in explanation.

AutoCAD

_____. (topic sentence)
Then he asked us to develop a campaign that includes images for billboards, print advertisements, and TV/radio advertisements. In our client's mind, a customer should be able to see, hear, smell, taste, and feel his product. So, we have to develop images that challenge the mind, that engage the senses. To help with this process, he has invited the staff to visit his restaurant tomorrow afternoon. Since this is our largest job to date, consider this project a priority.

Automotive Technology

_____. (topic sentence)
So, to test the intake air temperature sensor, allow the vehicle to cool. Use your hand to check the external temperature; if you can touch the engine, then it is safe to proceed. Next, use the scan tool to measure the intake air temperature. This reading should be close to the engine coolant temperature. If you smell burnt coolant fluid, check for leaks.

Criminal Justice

_____. (topic sentence)

And then, I found myself facing the much talked about wall, the wall that invites cadets to quit the academy. So immense, so intimidating, it stood higher than I could see—footholds protruding from bottom to top. With determination, I approached the wall, hand extended as if to pet a wild animal. The side felt cool, almost foreboding, against my palm. Both hands feeling the wall, I remembered that I have scaled many walls, faced many obstacles before, and this, this wall was just another one for me to conquer.

Electronics

_____. (topic sentence)

He waited a moment before trying the doorbell again. Once more, there was silence as he pushed the button. Perplexed, he opened the plate surrounding the button. Gently, he removed the button to examine the wire connections. To his dismay, he discovered that three of the wires appeared chewed. Replacing the button and cover, he decided to call the exterminators.

Information Technology

_____. (topic sentence)

So, the program closes whenever you open your Internet connection. To remedy this, open your control panel window which is located on the hard drive on the top, left hand corner of the screen. Next, open the Internet options menu window which is somewhere in the middle of your menu. Then, click on the cookies button and choose select all. Following this, delete the cookies; this should solve your problem.

Paralegal Studies

_____. (topic sentence)

Knowing how important this information is to the case, the assistant asked the client to describe the placement of the papers once again. The client reported leaving the papers on the desk to the right of his appointment book and to the left of his checkbook. To his recollection, no other items sat on the desk. The assistant noted that the client's description of the papers' location matched that of others in the house. This information, if truthful, is essential to the outcome of the case.

⤜ *EXERCISE 2.10* ⤛

In this exercise, the last sentence is missing. Write one that logically concludes the paragraph.

Allied Health

While writing her preliminary information, Mrs. Katz suddenly slumped forward dropping the clipboard and pen in front of her. The crash reverberated throughout the sparsely populated waiting room, alerting me of the incident. Immediately, I notified the doctor about her condition. Kneeling beside her, I checked her vital signs and noticed that her skin was cold and clammy. The doctor joined me and ordered me to contact the operating room. _____
_____. (concluding sentence)

AutoCAD

New to using AutoCAD, I hesitantly opened the drawing program on my computer. My eyes strained as I viewed the lesson that our instructor sent. Curious, I opened the tool-bar hunting for the pictures shown in the book. Nervous about making a mistake, I selected the first image in the assignment and chose the curve tool. To my amazement, the image changed to the curve that I wanted. _____
_____. (concluding sentence)

Automotive Technology

Engine whining like an impatient four-year old, the wheels crept onto the highway. "To coax this dinosaur to a service garage will take forever," she sighed. The front passenger side door refuses to close and the trunk pops open with every bump. As she begged the car to accelerate, the whining turned to grinding, loud and unpleasant. Finally, the service station appeared on the right, about a half mile down the road._____
_____. (concluding sentence)

Criminal Justice

The sirens sounded the alert for all residents to evacuate the area due to the impending storm. As the alert announced the evacuation, officers drove through nearly abandoned neighborhoods encouraging people to leave. Clouds hung heavy with water waiting to burst. Street by street, officers knocked on doors to announce the hurricane, urging people to leave. Despite the efforts, many people decided to stay with their homes. _____
_____. (concluding sentence)

Electronics

This incident upset many of us since Manuel practiced all of the safety techniques described in our handbook. From my position, I watched him climb the pole holding to the safety line. Once he reached the top, he tested the wire for activity. Unbeknownst to him, it must have still been active because in an instant, he fell from the pole. This occurred between 3:00 and 3:15 P.M. today. _____. (concluding sentence)

Information Technology

Shouting through the phone, the manager angrily stated that the email system was down once again. Without email, his team is unable to retrieve the information from another team across the country. To allay the manager's anger, the technician explained that the email system would be functional in an hour. Computer techs had added anti-spyware to protect the server from outside attack. _____
_____. (concluding sentence)

Paralegal Studies

Thinking over the two years of her paralegal study, Sharon considered the lessons learned. The pen felt tight in her hand as she reflected upon the long hours of focused study that earned her this opportunity. Many tried to describe this moment to her; none of the descriptions matched the excitement mixed with nervousness that filled her. Memories of past beginnings flooded her mind as she stood to smooth her skirt. Ignoring her beating heart, she opened her office door to greet her first client. _____
_____. (concluding sentence)

❧ EXERCISE 2.11 ❧

Now that you have practiced writing topic and concluding sentences, write both for the next exercise. To do this, add necessary information to introduce and to close the paragraph.

Allied Health

_____.

Install safety railings in the shower stall so that they are opposite each other. This placement will allow her to bathe while holding one of the rails at a time. To make this even safer, place rubber skids on the bottom of the tub; be sure that there are enough for her to step on. If there is room, add a corner bench so that she can rest as she bathes. _____
_____.

AutoCAD

_____.

To accommodate this, we will have to move the extra bedroom to the back of the house to the left of porch. The dimensions of the room will have to change to accommodate that placement. Another option is to place that bedroom to the right of the porch attached to the front bedroom. As soon as you have made your decision, notify me so that I can draft the revisions.

_____

_____.

Automotive Technology

_____.

Then, I will have time to complete the work on your car. It has been busy all day and with so many people here, I have not been able to even diagnose the problem to provide you with an estimate. I know how desperately you want your car returned. _____

_____.

Criminal Justice

_____.

And then, I accelerated to stay behind the escaping car. The radio crackled on the seat next to me, asking for an update of my surveillance. Keeping my eyes focused on the winding road, I fumbled to find the button to push to report my progress. My fingers gently brushed the side of the radio searching for the proper button. _____

_____.

Electronics

_____.

Then, the radiant bands of red and orange danced from one end of the globe to the other. Flashes of blue and green occasionally sprang from the base creating the effect of a virtual fire. To test the sensitivity of the light, I gently brushed the globe. As expected, the bands of color reacted to my touch, jumping to meet my contact._____

_____.

Information Technology

_____.

And then, we smelled burning plastic from the server. There were no visible flames that we could see; however, there was definitely an electrical fire. Immediately, all employees saved whatever data possible and turned off their machines. Now, we need your assistance in restoring whatever information that you can retrieve from the server._____

_____.

From the street, it appeared that someone might be home; a light flickered from within. Needing this interview, I decided to stand watch all night if necessary. Cautiously, I approached the door and readied to knock when I heard noises from the driveway. I turned sharply to see two men facing each other reflected in the street light. _____

_____.

⤳ *EXERCISE 2.12* ⤳

The challenge in writing an effective description is to have a clear understanding of what you intend to describe before attempting to write. Write a paragraph using descriptive details related to your five senses (sight, hearing, touch, taste, smell).

Topic: **Describe a time when you tried to solve a problem without first gathering all the needed information. What was the outcome?**

_____

_____

_____

_____

_____

_____

_____

_____

_____

_____

_____

_____

_____

_____

Chapter 3
Logical Connections

Illustrative Writing

TIPS

Definition

Illustrative writing provides the reader with one or more examples to illustrate a point. This form of writing is concrete, inviting the reader to see the same picture as the writer. Use vivid adjectives to create a visual example of your statement, idea, or point.

Career Uses

Use illustrative writing when writing a proposal requesting the need for more money or staff. Specific instances cited will strengthen any chances of gaining added resources. When bidding on work, include details that invite the potential customer to envision the finished product.

Principles of Illustrative Writing

How do you know when to use illustrative writing? Look for these types of questions or prompts:

- *Write a proposal that asks for . . .*

- *How would you complete . . .*

- *Give an example of . . .*

When asked to write an illustrative essay, create a list of adjectives or examples that will be included in the writing. Once you have developed this list, write a topic sentence and outline, being certain to add the specific example or examples to illustrate your point. The key to writing a strong illustrative essay is to use concrete examples of each of the presented points.

Avoid these Common Mistakes

Here are some of the common mistakes made by writers when using illustrative style:

- *Trying to illustrate an idea using general information*

- *Not writing a clear example: confusing one idea with another*

- *Using examples that do not correspond to the topic sentence*

- *Using abstract language instead of concrete language*

EXERCISES

⟨ *EXERCISE 3.1* ⟩

One of the purposes of illustrative writing is to describe an item or an idea using concrete language and specific detail. For this exercise, replace the given word with one or two specific examples. For example, bird—canary, parakeet, pigeon

Allied Health

1. teeth: _____

2. patient care: _____

3. allied health: _____

4. doctor: _____

5. instrument: _____

AutoCAD

1. drawing: _____

2. surface generation: _____

3. model: _____

4. project: _____

5. surface properties: _____

Automotive Technology

1. wrench: _____

2. screwdriver: _____

3. socket: _____

4. tires: _____

5. car: _____

Criminal Justice

1. law: _____

2. misdemeanor: _____

3. jail: _____

4. officer: _____

5. offender: _____

Electronics

1. tools: _____

2. power reader: _____

3. electrical charge: _____

4. circuit: _____

5. filters: _____

Information Technology

1. computer: _____

2. modem: _____

3. virus: _____

4. online connection: _____

5. printer: _____

Paralegal Studies

1. law: _____

2. criminal charge: _____

3. civil case: _____

4. wills: _____

5. legal documents: _____

Illustrative writing paints pictures using words. To emphasize a point, clear language describes a scene, object, procedure, or situation. For this exercise, practice visualizing the subject by drawing a picture of it in the space provided. Use your imagination and add as many details as you can; do not worry about the quality of your drawing. The exercise focuses your ability to describe something in detail.

Allied Health

Draw a picture either of the skeletal system or of an instrument layout for surgery.

AutoCAD

Draw a picture of an architectural layout or of an animation.

Automotive

Draw a picture of an engine from whatever perspective you desire.

Criminal Justice

Draw a layout of the crime scene of your choice.

Electronics

Draw the schemata of a circuit board.

Information Technology

Draw a picture of the connections between a printer, computer, and television.

Paralegal Studies

Draw a picture of a standard courtroom layout.

❦ *EXERCISE 3.3* ❧

In this exercise, change the sentences to make them illustrative: replace general language with more specific language. For example,

The bird flew from the pole to the nest without flapping its wings.
The eagle glided through the air from the telephone pole to the large nest housed in the tree.

Allied Health

1. His tooth hurt this morning when he awoke.

2. To increase patient satisfaction, we need to increase patient care.

3. She is going to college to study allied health.

4. After his accident, Jack made many doctor appointments.

5. Please ready the instruments for the doctor.

_____

_____

_____

_____

AutoCAD

1. Your drawings are absolutely fantastic!

2. In order to complete this phase of the project, you need to add surface generation to the model.

3. When will your project be completed?

4. His model shows the potential problems with the design; it needs to be modified before the presentation next week.

5. Janet believes that the surface properties of the drawing are perfect for the plans.

_____

_____

_____

_____

Automotive Technology

1. When changing a tire, use a wrench to loosen the wheel.

2. Please pass me the screwdriver that is on the bench.

3. In order for us to fix the oil pan, we need a socket set.

4. The customer requested a set of new tires.

5. Roberto decided to purchase a new car.

_____

_____

_____

_____

Criminal Justice

1. The woman broke the law.

2. Last night, the juvenile committed a misdemeanor.

3. He called from jail, however I do not remember which one.

4. From her studies in criminal justice, she decided to become an officer.

5. Your offender group will meet in the large group room this afternoon.

_____

_____

_____

_____

Electronics

1. Please, bring your tools with you because the dryer is experiencing power surges.

2. Can you use your power reader in order to determine where the faulty wire is located?

3. To test for an electrical charge, I need to turn off the circuit breaker so that I can check the connections.

4. Check the power cord; maybe there is something wrong with it.

5. The filter allows the signal to travel without losing too much power.

_____

_____

_____

_____

Information Technology

1. Marcus wants to buy a new computer.

2. The modem is running slower than usual.

3. Beware, there is a virus running through the company's server.

4. His online connection is much quicker now.

5. Maria connected the printer to the computer even though she does not have a driver for it.

_____

_____

_____

_____

Paralegal Studies

1. Jason decided to study paralegal studies because of his interest in the law.

2. Her client, despite his protestations, was charged with a crime.

3. Because he refused to fulfill his contract, he must face a civil lawsuit.

4. No one is certain as to whether he left a will or not.

5. The legal documents will be ready for you in the morning by 10:00.

_____

_____

_____

_____

❧ *EXERCISE 3.4* ☙

For this exercise, choose one of the sentences from EXERCISE 3 or create another. Use it as a topic sentence, then write a paragraph providing detail to support your subject. In the example below, the topic sentence is at the end instead of the beginning. For example,

The eagle glided through the air from the telephone pole to the large nest housed in the tree. Once there, the eagle perched stoically on the edge, as if to wait. For what, I did not know. We waited, he and I, and then suddenly from the corner of the horizon soared a second eagle, mimicking the same gallant manner as the first. Within moments, the eagles joined each other, in tandem, as they took to the air towards the mountain leaving me with the impression of their grace. Eagles are, indeed, the most regal of all birds.

Allied Health

_____

_____

_____

_____

_____

_____

AutoCAD

_____

_____

_____

_____

_____

_____

Automotive

_____

_____

_____

_____

_____

_____

Criminal Justice

_____

_____

_____

_____

_____

_____

Electronics

_____

_____

_____

_____

_____

_____

Information Technology

_____

_____

_____

_____

_____

_____

Paralegal Studies

_____

_____

_____

_____

_____

_____

Cause and Effect Writing

TIPS

Definition

Cause and Effect writing provides reasons and explanations for events, conditions, or behavior allowing for understanding of connections. This form of writing uses a clear format: describe the condition or event and then report the possible outcomes using chronological reasoning. Some cause and effect essays use a reverse chronological format starting with the effect first. Whichever chronology is used, strong essays contain transitions and signal words (as a result, due to, possibly) that show the association between the condition and outcome.

Career Uses

Use cause and effect essay form when reporting a problem or potential problem to a supervisor or consumer. You will use this format each time that you need to report a problem to someone or try to explain the reason for a situation. This writing style is a common form used in the workplace.

Principles of Cause and Effect Writing

How do you know when to use cause and effect writing? Look for these types of questions or prompts:

- *Explain the effects of . . .*

- *Think about _____. What caused _____?*

- *Why are you such a _____?*

- *What are the signs of _____? How can this be prevented?*

- *What are the causes of _____?*

- *Should _____ be allowed _____?*

When asked to write a cause and effect essay, describe the condition or event before listing the existing or possible effects. This format is clear because it logically maps the writer's reasoning, allowing the reader to understand the premise. After writing a strong thesis statement, use transitions to move the writing from one point to another so that the reader can easily follow the logic. Use transitions that show chronology such as therefore, next, and following.

To determine the relationship between the cause and the effect, writers use a diagram as a basis for linking elements. For example,

Excellent study skills ⟶ Good grades

action (cause) result of study (effect)

In order to show that the use of strong study habits results in good grades, the writer must use a clear thesis followed by specific details to convince the reader to study harder. To properly establish this relationship, the writer needs to consider as many connections as possible between the cause and effect.

Avoid these Common Mistakes

Here are some of the common mistakes made by writers when using cause and effect style:

- *Emphasizing only one cause when others of the same importance may exist*

- *Incorrect assumption of a causal relationship*

- *Writing the details before establishing the relationship between the elements*

EXERCISES

⤜ *EXERCISE 3.5* ⤛

Cause and effect sentences consist of two parts: a cause and the result of the cause (effect). In the space provided next to each item number, write which part is missing from the sentence. Once you have decided whether the cause or the effect is missing, complete the sentence. Be careful, cause and effect statements do not always follow the same order (cause followed by an effect). For example,

> **Cause** **Eating too much food and not exercising.**

> **Effect** **results in unhealthy weight gain.**

Allied Health

_____ 1. Better health care is a result of _____.

_____ 2. All surgical technicians attended the training, meaning _____.

_____ 3. Dental hygienists must pass a licensing test before they can _____.

_____ 4. _____, which created an overcrowded waiting room.

_____ 5. If you do not floss regularly _____.

_____ 6. _____ you have caught a cold.

_____ 7. _____ he faints.

_____ 8. The board granted two million dollars for the project due to _____.

_____ 9. Drugs that are stimulants _____.

_____10. Untreated high blood pressure_____.

AutoCAD

_____ 1. When you slice a solid in half, _____.

_____ 2. _____ allowing the designer to see many surfaces at once.

_____ 3. The design team loved her drawings; _____.

_____ 4. Once you have specified the X-axis coordinates _____.

_____ 5. _____, which results in a quality design.

_____ 6. _____; that is the purpose for moving the room to the other side of the house.

_____ 7. All of the hours spent studying _____.

_____ 8. _____ and now the customer is pleased.

_____ 9. _____, which is the reason for the shape of the final product.

_____10. Following the procedure for inserting blocks _____.

Automotive Technology

_____ 1. _____ leaving the tire over pressurized.

_____ 2. The calipers were installed upside down meaning _____.

_____ 3. _____ now the whole steering system must be replaced.

_____ 4. If you do not change your oil regularly, _____.

_____ 5. Worn shock absorbers cause _____.

_____ 6. _____ because the fluid overflows when it becomes hot.

_____ 7. _____ results in longer life for the transmission.

_____ 8. It is important to keep the gas tank filled above the quarter tank mark because

_____.

_____ 9. You'll know when a cylinder head gasket has blown because _____.

_____10. _____ or the brake fluid will boil and cause the

brake pedal to go soft.

Criminal Justice

_____ 1. _____ leads to a decrease in street crime.

_____ 2. The forensic psychologist will write a profile of Jared which _____

_____.

_____ 3. Working too many long shifts without taking breaks can cause _____

_____.

_____ 4. New victims rights resulted from _____.

_____ 5. _____ beginning next year, alternative sanctions will be

assigned when applicable.

_____ 6. New security measures implemented in airports _____.

_____ 7. Community policing is the most effective measure for reducing crime because ___

_____.

_____ 8. _____ meaning that he will leave the

detention center next week.

_____ 9. _____ raising drug crimes significantly.

_____10. The school resource officer began an incentive program for students who attend

the most classes in a quarter, so far _____.

Electronics

_____ 1. Due to his hard work on his final electronics project, _____.

_____ 2. _____ is caused by charge and discharge of the capacitor.

_____ 3. _____ which caused the circuit to short.

_____ 4. Now that the job is complete, _____.

_____ 5. _____ then the components will be properly connected.

_____ **6.** _____ is caused by the larger sized resistor.

_____ **7.** _____ results in the radio not working.

_____ **8.** _____, which explains the occasional dip in power.

_____ **9.** _____ so that the object loses its magnetic charge.

_____**10.** Inductive reactance causes _____.

Information Technology

_____ **1.** _____ meaning that no one in the company had access to intranet services.

_____ **2.** New spyware detects adware and malicious trojan applications resulting _____
_____.

_____ **3.** Be sure to back up all of your software files or else _____.

_____ **4.** _____ and now the program crashes each time the computer starts up.

_____ **5.** _____ so the computers can now communicate with the company's phone system.

_____ **6.** _____ sending the message to everyone on the general mailing list instead.

_____ **7.** He finished installing the wireless system in the café so that _____
_____.

_____ **8.** If you maintain only one customer database, _____.

_____ **9.** _____ increased the productivity in the factory by fifty percent.

_____**10.** The technology team presented their proposition well this morning, _____
_____.

Paralegal Studies

_____ **1.** The judge moved up the time of the trial and now _____.

_____ **2.** The law firm decided to add three more legal assistants to the firm, which _____
_____.

_____ **3.** _____ resulting in a change of the abortion laws.

_____ 4. _____ the remaining parent retains custody of the minor children.

_____ 5. Long hours of research and study _____.

_____ 6. The defense was illogical and not well-researched, which _____
_____.

_____ 7. _____ which prompted the attorney to file an appeal.

_____ 8. According to the client, the contractor breached contract leading _____.

_____ 9. _____ resulting in foreclosure at the end of the day.

_____ 10. At three o'clock, Roger was served with a subpoena meaning _____
_____.

❧ *EXERCISE 3.6* ❧

Write a paragraph that introduces the given cause and effect. Be sure to include some details that strengthen your position. For example,

Cause: **regular study of class material**
Effect: **high grades and better retention**

When you devote an hour a day for study, you will earn high grades and retain more information. Many studies indicate that the human brain is better able to learn, analyze, retain, and apply information when it has had daily exposure to it. Furthermore, the information is stored in long-term memory after it has been applied in life. The same studies show that exposing the brain to the information only once before an exam is not enough.

Allied Health

1. Cause: untreated diabetes
   Effect: can kill

_____

_____

_____

_____

2. Cause: hand washing

   Effect: kills germs after contact with each patient

_____

_____

_____

_____

AutoCAD

1. Cause: the design team loved her drawings

   Effect: she was hired as the lead designer for the project

_____

_____

_____

_____

2. Cause: use of the surface tool

   Effect: allows the architect to change surfaces many times before selecting one

_____

_____

_____

_____

Automotive Technology

1. Cause: timely oil changes

   Effect: longer engine life

_____

_____

_____

_____

2. Cause: low tire pressure

   Effect: damaged rims and need for new tires

_____

_____

_____

_____

Criminal Justice

1. Cause: increased crime in a neighborhood
   Effect: more officers assigned to police the area

   _____

   _____

   _____

   _____

   _____

2. Cause: creation of youth recreation programs
   Effect: lower rate of after school crimes committed

   _____

   _____

   _____

   _____

   _____

Electronics

1. Cause: spilled coffee on the computer keyboard
   Effect: circuit short so that the keyboard does not work

   _____

   _____

   _____

   _____

   _____

2. Cause: broken heating element in a water heater
   Effect: no hot water

   _____

   _____

   _____

   _____

   _____

Information Technology

1. Cause: virus in the server

   Effect: attacks the company email software

   _____

   _____

   _____

   _____

   _____

2. Cause: back up files daily

   Effect: less chance of losing all work

   _____

   _____

   _____

   _____

   _____

Paralegal Studies

1. Cause: judge moved the trial up three days

   Effect: less time to prepare for opening statements

   _____

   _____

   _____

   _____

   _____

2. Cause: arrested for cruelty to animals

   Effect: trial to prove guilt

   _____

   _____

   _____

   _____

   _____

✿ EXERCISE 3.7 ✿

Choose one of the examples from the previous exercise to expand. In the space provided below, write an essay using your introductory paragraph. Add more detail for paragraphs two and three to help the reader to understand your opening statement. Conclude with a fourth paragraph that summarizes your main points.

Classification Writing

TIPS

Definition

Classification writing describes types of people, items, or situations. The purpose of this style is to combine specific items into general groupings. Writers create groups according to the presence of a common characteristic such as color, use, or style.

Career Uses

In the workplace, use classification for reports that require groupings of items or ideas. This type of writing is present in proposal or project writing.

Principles of Classification Writing

How do you know when to use classification writing? Look for these types of questions or prompts:

- *Explain the three types of political parties in the United States.*

- *Write an essay discussing two types of energy resources.*

When you are asked to describe, list, or explain two or more of anything, write a classification essay. Since the purpose of classification is to structure information into logical categories, define the category first.

Avoid these Common Mistakes

Here are some of the common mistakes made by writers when using classification style.

- *Your classification should focus on only one kind of grouping. Avoid mixing two classifications together.*

- *Understand the classification that you are using for description.*

- *Use general categories rather than specific ones.*

EXERCISES

⟨ EXERCISE 3.8 ⟩

For this exercise, classify the following groups of words; be specific. For example,

Round fruit

- **apple**
- **orange**
- **peach**
- **grapefruit**

1. _____

   triangle
   square
   rectangle
   hexagon

2. _____

   station wagon
   coupe
   pick up truck
   sedan

3. _____

   police officer
   immigration officer
   security guard
   airport screeners

4. _____

   kitten
   puppy
   calf
   infant

5. _____

    purple

    orange

    green

    brown

6. _____

    wrench

    hammer

    screwdriver

    pliers

7. _____

    crayon

    pencil

    pen

    marker

8. _____

    comedy

    tragedy

    romance

    adventure

9. _____

    classical

    reggae

    rhythm & blues

    country

10. _____

    kitchen

    end

    card

    console

Write a sentence indicating the relationship between the two objects listed. For example,
  <u>**pear, apple:**</u>
  <u>**Apples and pears are both fruits that are traditionally available in the winter.**</u>

Allied Health

1. aneroid, mercury

_____

_____

2. mask, latex gloves

_____

_____

AutoCAD

1. dash, long-dash dot

_____

_____

2. DIMEDIT, DIMTEDIT

_____

_____

Automotive

1. fuse replacement method, circuit breaker method

_____

_____

2. V4, V8

_____

_____

Criminal Justice

1. selective incapacitation, collective incapacitation

_____

_____

2. community court, federal court

_____

_____

Electronics

1. analog, digital

_____

_____

2. parallel, series

_____

_____

Information Technology

1. use of greater chip density, accelerator board

_____

_____

2. network infrastructure, component infrastructure

_____

_____

Paralegal Studies

1. summons, complaint/original petition

_____

_____

2. birth certificate, marriage license

_____

_____

For this exercise, choose one of your sentences from the above exercise to use as a topic sentence. Write an introductory paragraph of four or five sentences. Be sure to explain how the items introduced are classified and how they're used according to the grouping. For example,

> Apples and pears are both fruits that are traditionally available in the winter. During the winter season, these fruit are ready for harvest and therefore, are freshest. Winter fruits contain more fiber than summer ones such as peaches and plums. For this reason, they survive the colder weather of the northern states in the United States.

Allied Health

_____
_____
_____
_____
_____
_____

AutoCAD

_____
_____
_____
_____
_____
_____

Automotive

_____
_____
_____
_____
_____
_____

Criminal Justice

_____

_____

_____

_____

_____

_____

Electronics

_____

_____

_____

_____

_____

_____

Information Technology

_____

_____

_____

_____

_____

_____

Paralegal Studies

_____

_____

_____

_____

_____

_____

Write a five-paragraph essay using the introductory paragraph that you wrote in the previous exercise. Paragraphs two through four should elaborate on your classification with the last paragraph used as a conclusion. You may need do some research about your classification in order to use enough specific detail.

_____

_____

_____

_____

_____

_____

_____

_____

_____

_____

_____

_____

_____

_____

_____

_____

_____

_____

_____

_____

_____

_____

_____

_____

_____

_____

_____

_____

_____

_____

_____

_____

_____

Comparison/Contrast Writing

TIPS

Definition

Comparison/Contrast writing compares and/or contrasts two or more items, events, ideas, or people. Two writing methods express this relationship: block arrangement and point-by-point. Use block arrangement when describing a broad picture in a short essay or when examining an uncomplicated issue. Use the point-by-point method when focusing on details in a long essay or when examining complex issues.

Career Uses

Use comparison/contrast writing for proposals requesting the addition of resources such as equipment or staff. In addition, supervisors utilize this form for report writing when stating an opinion of policy change. Writers also use comparison/contrast writing to present two or more choices to work-groups so that decisions can be made through an examination of similarities and/or differences.

Principles of Comparison/Contrast Writing

How do you know when to use comparison/contrast writing? Look for these types of questions or prompts:

- *Explain the differences between . . .*

- *Compare X with Y . . .*

- *Contrast X with Y . . .*

- *What are the similarities between . . .*

- *List the differences between . . .*

When asked to compare or contrast information, use the comparison/contrast writing style which clearly illustrates similarities and differences between ideas, people, events, and items. Use two standard patterns to organize ideas: *block arrangement* and *point-by-point arrangement*. If one writes of the differences between cars and trucks using a block arrangement, the first paragraph will discuss cars while the second discusses trucks. If one writes of the differences between cars and trucks using point-by-point arrangement, the first paragraph will discuss a point about each. For example, they have different body styles.

A comparison/contrast essay can discuss similarities, differences, or both depending on the material and the purpose of the essay. Regardless of the format or organization, a strong comparison/contrast essay contains transitions to connect ideas. For example, in contrast, similarly, but, on the other hand, also. These words show the reader the relationship between ideas.

Avoid these Common Mistakes

Here are some of the common mistakes made by writers when using comparison/contrast style:

- *Choose to write about two subjects that share some common features.*

- *Do not write about one item, person, or event without mentioning the another.*

- *Use either point-by-point or block arrangement, not both.*

EXERCISES

⟨ *EXERCISE 3.12* ⟩

For each of these topics, list all of the similarities and differences you can. You may list words or phrases under each of the columns. For example,

Owning a cat vs. Owning a dog

Similarities	Differences
both are domesticated animals	they are members of different species
they are capable of getting along with other domesticated animals	cats are more independent than dogs
	dogs require walking/time outside
they can be wonderful companions	dogs are more loyal to their owners
they are popular pets	cats are less work as pets
they need assistance with basic needs	

Allied Health

Topic A

Working in a doctor's/dentist's office vs. Working in a hospital

Similarities	*Differences*

87

Topic B

Working as a per diem employee vs. Working as a fixed shift employee

Similarities	Differences

AutoCAD

Topic A

2D Drawing vs. 3D Rendering

Similarities	Differences

Topic B

Working for a company, agency or business vs. Working as a contractor

Similarities	Differences

Automotive Technology

Topic A

V4 engines vs. V8 engines

Similarities	Differences

Topic B

Manual transmission vs. Automatic transmission

Similarities	Differences

Criminal Justice

Topic A

Working for a security company vs. Working for the police force

Similarities	Differences

Topic B

Jails vs. Prisons

Similarities	Differences

Electronics

Topic A

AC power vs. DC power

Similarities	Differences

Topic B

Electrical contracting vs. Working as a lineman

Similarities	Differences

Information Technology

Topic A

Windows vs. Macintosh

Similarities	Differences

Topic B

Dial up Internet vs. DSL Internet

Similarities	Differences

Paralegal Studies

Topic A

Real estate law vs. Criminal law

Similarities	Differences

Topic B

Working in a small law firm vs. Working in a large law firm

Similarities	Differences

❧ *EXERCISE 3.13* ❧

Using the list of similarities from EXERCISE 3.12, for each example below, write a paragraph that compares each of the two items. For example,

<u>Topic:</u> Owning a cat v. Owning a dog

<u>Similarities:</u> domesticated, capable of getting along with other pets, popular, need assistance with basic needs

Cats and dogs share many of the same qualities as pets. For example, most breeds of dogs and cats are domesticated. In addition, both enjoy the company of other pets. Best of all, cats and dogs make wonderful companions due to their loyalty to their owners.

Allied Health

Topic A: Working in a doctor's/dentist's office vs. Working in a hospital

Similarities: _____

_____

Write your paragraph in the space below.

_____

_____

_____

_____

Topic B: Working as a per diem employee vs. Working as a fixed shift employee
Similarities: _____

_____

Write your paragraph in the space below.

_____

_____

_____

_____

AutoCAD
Topic A: 2D Drawing vs. 3D rendering
Similarities: _____

_____

Write your paragraph in the space below.

_____

_____

_____

_____

Topic B: Working for a company, agency or business vs. Working as a contractor
Similarities: _____

_____

Write your paragraph in the space below.

_____

_____

_____

_____

Automotive

Topic A: V4 engines vs. V8 engines

Similarities: _____

_____

Write your paragraph in the space below.

_____

_____

_____

_____

Topic B: Manual transmissions vs. Automatic transmissions

Similarities: _____

_____

Write your paragraph in the space below.

_____

_____

_____

_____

Criminal Justice

Topic A: Working for a security company vs. Working for a police force

Similarities: _____

_____

Write your paragraph in the space below.

_____

_____

_____

_____

Topic B: Jails vs. Prisons

Similarities: _____

_____

Write your paragraph in the space below.

_____

_____

_____

_____

Electronics

Topic A: AC power vs. DC power

Similarities: _____

_____

Write your paragraph in the space below

_____

_____

_____

_____

Topic B: Electrical contracting vs. Working as a lineman

Similarities: _____

_____

Write your paragraph in the space below.

_____

_____

_____

_____

Information Technology

Topic A: Windows vs. Macintosh

Similarities: _____

_____

Write your paragraph in the space below.

_____

_____

_____

_____

Topic B: Dial up Internet vs. DSL Internet

Similarities: _____

_____

Write your paragraph in the space below.

_____

_____

_____

_____

Paralegal Studies

Topic A: Real estate law vs. Criminal law

Similarities: _____

_____

Write your paragraph in the space below.

_____

_____

_____

_____

Topic B: Working in a small law firm vs. Working in a large law firm

Similarities: _____

_____

Write your paragraph in the space below.

_____

_____

_____

_____

Using the list of differences from EXERCISE 3.12, for each example below, write a paragraph that contrasts each of the two items. For example,

> <u>Topic:</u> Owning a cat vs. Owning a dog
>
> <u>Differences:</u> different species, independent-dependent, outdoor requirements, ease of ownership
>
> While cats and dogs have some similarities, key differences must be examined when considering them as pets. Cats are more independent than dogs meaning that they do not require as much work from their owners. However, due to a dog's dependence on his/her owner, the dog is a more loyal pet than a cat. The prospective owner must assess the amount of time needed for pet care before choosing between a cat or a dog.

Allied Health

Topic A: Working in a doctor's/dentist's office vs. Working in a hospital

Differences: _____

_____

Write your paragraph in the space below.

_____

_____

_____

_____

Topic B: Working as a per diem employee vs. Working as a fixed shift employee

Differences: _____

_____

Write your paragraph in the space below.

_____

_____

_____

_____

AutoCAD

Topic A: 2D Drawing vs. 3D Rendering

Differences: _____

_____

Write your paragraph in the space below.

_____

_____

_____

_____

Topic B: Working for a company, agency or business vs. Working as a contractor

Differences: _____

_____

Write your paragraph in the space below.

_____

_____

_____

_____

Automotive

Topic A: V4 engines vs. V8 engines

Differences: _____

_____

Write your paragraph in the space below.

_____

_____

_____

_____

Topic B: Manual transmission vs. Automatic transmission

Differences: _____

_____

Write your paragraph in the space below.

_____

_____

_____

_____

Criminal Justice

Topic A: Working for a security company vs. Working for a police force

Differences: _____

_____

Write your paragraph in the space below.

_____

_____

_____

_____

Topic B: Jails vs. Prisons

Differences: _____

_____

Write your paragraph in the space below.

_____

_____

_____

_____

Electronics

Topic A: AC power vs. DC power

Differences: _____

_____

Write your paragraph in the space below.

_____

_____

_____

_____

Topic B: Electrical contracting vs. Working as a lineman

Differences: _____

_____

Write your paragraph in the space below.

_____

_____

_____

_____

Information Technology

Topic A: Windows vs. Macintosh

Differences: _____

_____

Write your paragraph in the space below.

_____

_____

_____

_____

Topic B: Dial-up Internet vs. DSL Internet

Differences: _____

_____

Write your paragraph in the space below.

_____

_____

_____

_____

Paralegal Studies

Topic A: Real Estate law vs. Criminal law

Differences: _____

_____

Write your paragraph in the space below.

_____

_____

_____

_____

Topic B: Working in a small law firm vs. Working in a large law firm

Differences: _____

_____

Write your paragraph in the space below.

_____

_____

_____

_____

Now that you have practiced writing comparisons and contrasts between two subjects, decide on a topic and write an essay. In your essay, either compare or contrast qualities between your subjects. Be sure to use transitional phrases to strengthen your writing.

_____

_____

_____

_____

_____

EXERCISE 3.16

Consider the essay you wrote in Exercise 3.15; re-write the essay to include both comparisons and contrasts using either point-by-point or block arrangement organization.

104

Process Writing

TIPS

Definition

Process writing provides the reader with information that explains how to do something or how something works. A well-written process essay leads the reader through logical steps in order to complete a task. Each direction supplies the reader with valuable detail designed to allow for completion of one step before progressing to the next. There are two types of process papers: fixed and loose processes.

Career Uses

Use process writing when writing manuals or handbooks for employee training. Whenever a worker needs to duplicate someone's product, he/she will need to read the process manual. Manuals for repair of machines or for describing complex procedures, which are both fixed processes, are most successful when written in process writing style.

Principles of Process Writing

How do you know when to use process writing? Look for these types of questions or prompts:

- *Explain how to . . .*

- *Describe the process of . . .*

- *Tell how _____ works*

- *How do you _____?*

- *How does _____ work?*

When asked to write a process essay, prepare your outline paying attention to list all required materials to complete the task. Once the materials are listed, describe the steps in logical order. Fixed processes are those that require a specific order of tasks or events to be completed properly. Loose processes are those that have a general order of tasks or events that can vary slightly depending on the situation. For both types, write an outline, which organizes the steps, then complete the description using specific detail.

Avoid these Common Mistakes

Here are some of the common mistakes made by writers when using process writing style:

- *Poorly organized steps which confuse the reader*

- *Failure to list needed materials in the beginning of the essay*

- *Too many details that overpower the steps*

- *Writing opinion rather than using facts*

EXERCISES

<3 *EXERCISE 3.17* &>

For each of the examples below, list all of the materials or supplies for the named task (imagine that you are going to write a process essay for a manual). What materials or knowledge would the reader need to successfully complete the task? For example,

> Process: Recipe for making homemade chocolate chip cookies
> List of materials needed: oven, mixing bowl, wooden spoon, baking sheet, flour, sugar, egg, water, chocolate chips, baking soda, salt, butter

Allied Health

Process: Sterilizing instruments before use

List of materials needed: _____

_____

_____

AutoCAD

Process: Creating a scene for a model

List of materials needed: _____

_____

_____

Automotive

Process: Changing a tire on a car

List of materials needed: _____

_____

_____

Criminal Justice

Process: Arresting an offender

List of materials needed: _____

_____

_____

Electronics

Process: Reading a digital multimeter

List of materials needed: _____

_____

_____

Information Technology

Process: Burning a CD

List of materials needed: _____

_____

_____

Paralegal Studies

Process: Filing a petition for the dissolution of marriage

List of materials needed: _____

_____

_____

❖ *EXERCISE 3.18* ❖

Using the process and list of materials from EXERCISE 1, write two sentences: one introduces your process and one lists the materials needed. For example,

> <u>Process:</u> **Baking chocolate chip cookies**
>
> <u>Introduction:</u> **When was the last time that you bit into a hot, gooey, fresh-from-the-oven, chocolate chip cookie? To bake the best chocolate chip cookies, you will need to assemble the following materials: oven, mixing bowl, wooden spoon, baking sheet, flour, sugar, egg, water, chocolate chips, baking soda, salt, and butter.**

Allied Health

Process: Sterilizing instruments before use

Introduction: _____

_____

_____

AutoCAD

Process: Creating a scene for a model

Introduction: _____

_____

_____

Automotive Technology

Process: Changing a flat tire

Introduction: _____

_____

_____

Criminal Justice

Process: Arresting an offender

Introduction: _____

_____

_____

Electronics

Process: Reading a digital multimeter

Introduction: _____

_____

_____

Information Technology

Process: Burning a CD

Introduction: _____

_____

_____

Paralegal Studies

Process: Dissolution of a marriage

Introduction: _____

_____

_____

When writing process essays, it is important to know the steps involved. In this exercise, choose a process from your field then list the steps in order. The object is to write your directions so that the reader can duplicate your process. For example, if you are studying automotive technology, you may decide to list the steps for an engine oil change. For example,

<u>Process:</u> Washing a car

<u>Steps:</u>
1. Collect all the needed materials.
2. Rinse the car with warm water.
3. Using a brush, scrub the tires.
4. Soap the car using a sponge.
5. Rinse the car spraying water from top to bottom.
6. Gently dry the car with a clean, white cloth.

Allied Health

Process: _____

Steps: _____

_____

_____

_____

_____

_____

AutoCAD

Process: _____

Steps: _____

_____

_____

_____

_____

_____

Automotive Technology

Process: _____

Steps: _____

_____

_____

_____

_____

Criminal Justice

Process: _____

Steps: _____

_____

_____

_____

_____

Electronics

Process: _____

Steps: _____

_____

_____

_____

_____

Information Technology

Process: _____

Steps: _____

_____

_____

_____

_____

Paralegal Studies

Process: _____

Steps: _____

_____

_____

_____

_____

For the next exercise, rewrite the sentences so that they reflect the process writing style. Add details to change the sentences. Do not try to list all of the materials and steps in each sentence. For example,

> **To write a process essay, collect your information, outline your notes, write a draft using specific detail, and proofread it.**

Allied Health

1. Chart a patient's progress.

2. Check a patient's blood pressure.

3. Use universal precautions when working with all patients.

_____

_____

_____

AutoCAD

1. Render a figure.

2. Add a gradient to the design, so that it matches that of the yard.

3. Animate the buttons of a webpage.

_____

_____

_____

Automotive Technology

1. Change the oil in the car.

2. Check the charge in a car battery.

3. Check the air pressure in the tires.

_____

_____

_____

Criminal Justice

1. Write an arrest report.

2. Dust a door for fingerprints.

3. Write an abuse report.

_____

_____

_____

Electronics

1. Check the ground of a wire.

2. Test a circuit breaker for power.

3. Measure the input voltage response.

_____

_____

_____

Information Technology

1. Check for a modem connection.

2. Install a software program.

3. Print a document.

_____

_____

_____

Paralegal Studies

1. Write a closing statement for a house.

2. Prepare a complaint.

3. Research a case using law books.

_____

_____

_____

❦ *EXERCISE 3.21* ❧

Write a process essay that includes process materials, logical organization and details.

Allied Health

_____
_____
_____
_____
_____
_____
_____
_____
_____
_____
_____
_____
_____
_____
_____

AutoCAD

_____
_____
_____
_____
_____
_____
_____
_____
_____
_____
_____
_____
_____
_____
_____

Automotive Technology

Criminal Justice

Electronics

_____
_____
_____
_____
_____
_____
_____
_____
_____
_____
_____
_____
_____
_____
_____
_____
_____
_____

Information Technology

_____
_____
_____
_____
_____
_____
_____
_____
_____
_____
_____
_____
_____
_____
_____
_____
_____
_____

Chapter 4
Persuasion

Persuasive Writing

TIPS

Definition

Persuasive writing states an opinion or point of view then supports it using specific details. To effectively prove a case, the writer directs the words to the targeted audience with the hope that the reader will take action or change an opinion. Writers express their points of view using factual details and controlled emotion in an effort to convince the audience to believe as they do.

Career Uses

Use persuasive style when writing a proposal, whether it is for funds to start a business or to add programs or materials to existing businesses. Managers and business owners write persuasively whenever there is a need to refute an argument, for example, to address a customer's complaint. Grant applications and certain bank loans call for this style of writing as well.

Principles of Persuasive Writing

How do you know when to use persuasive writing? Look for these types of questions or prompts:

- *An opinion or statement is clearly presented which is then followed by a question asking the writer to choose a point of view to defend or dispute.*

- *Please write about your feelings of . . .*

- *Now that you have studied _____, write an essay stating and defending your position concerning this issue.*

When asked to write a persuasive essay, state the facts of the situation or case first then use specific details to defend your perspective. To strongly state your opinion, link your facts together using logical explanations of the relationships between facts. This form of writing requires the use of logical discussion with some controlled emotion. Writers express both fact and feeling about the topic. Remember that the objective in persuasive writing is to convince the reader to believe as the writer does.

Avoid these Common Mistakes

Here are some of the common mistakes made by writers when using persuasive style:

- *Do not switch points of views or opinions during the essay.* In the opening sentence, state your opinion or position about the topic. Do not switch opinions during the essay. This will weaken the writing and cloud your meaning. For example, if writing about the effects of television watching, do not state that all television viewing is harmful and then state later that some is harmful.

- *Do not confuse the perspective by introducing too many extra elements; add only information that strengthens the point of view.*

EXERCISES

⟨ EXERCISE 4.1 ⟩

Complete each sentence with a persuasive phrase. Be sure that your phrase fits the meaning of the sentence. For example,

I decided to enroll in college because _____.

I decided to enroll in college because I want to learn a different trade to change careers and increase my salary.

Allied Health

1. Last night the medical assistants decided to strike in response to _____

   _____

2. To earn the most money working in a hospital, you need _____

   _____

3. Emergency workers need to update training annually because _____

   _____

4. Incentives offered to those studying medicine are important to _____

   _____

5. It is important for all health care workers to wash hands _____

   _____

AutoCAD

1. To earn the most money for this project, _____

   _____

2. The 3D model indicates that there are many possibilities for improvement such as _____

   _____

3. Adding a slope to the yard is best for this design because _____

   _____

4. It is important to update rendering programs often since _____

   _____

5. I believe that this schematic is best suited for this kitchen because _____

   _____

Automotive Technology

1. I think that the transmission should be flushed now because _____

   _____

2. Due to the amount of oil leaking around the gasket, I think _____

   _____

3. That color yellow is not generally good on a car since _____

   _____

4. After checking the tire pressure, I believe that the front tires should be replaced due to___

   _____

5. I believe that the car needs new windshield wipers; it is necessary to have working ones

   when_____

Criminal Justice

1. Terrorism threats remains high now because _____

   _____

2. I believe that there is a need to hire more animal control officers due to _____

   _____

3. Officers need annual training in effective methods of handling domestic violence calls since _____

4. More car accidents occur at this intersection because _____
_____

5. Protective vests are an important piece of an officer's uniform since _____
_____

Electronics

1. To properly install a circuit breaker, one must _____
_____

2. It is dangerous for linemen to work in storm conditions because _____
_____

3. Before changing a wire, it is essential to test the wire first since _____
_____

4. When buying a gas generator, do not connect it to the wiring of the house because _____
_____

5. I think that it is better to work with a contracting team than alone due to _____
_____

Information Technology

1. In my opinion, laptops are better computers than desktops because _____
_____

2. It is important for information technologists to continue training in new software programs since _____

3. I believe that each computer needs to have at least two USB ports because _____
_____

4. Firewalls are the safest way to protect our system _____
_____

5. New DVD-ROM drives should replace the CD-ROM drives if _____
_____

Paralegal Studies

1. I think that all legal assistants and secretaries in our office earned a raise this quarter because _____

2. Mr. Jones deserves full compensation for his injuries due to _____

3. Identity theft cases are multiplying, I believe, as a result of _____

4. The state court will hear the case, I am certain, because of the _____

5. When I learned of the verdict, I was stunned; he did not deserve a prison sentence since _____

❧ EXERCISE 4.2 ❧

For each of the questions below, write a topic sentence that clearly states your point of view. Be sure to include both the issue and your position. For example,

Original Sentence: **With increasing college tuition costs, fewer people attend colleges and trade schools than in the past. To advance in your career, is more education required?**

Rewritten Sentence: **Even though the cost of attending trade school is increasing, I feel that it is essential for me to continue my studies because, in order to be promoted, I need a college degree.**

Allied Health

1. To save money, the hospital administrators decided to cut employee hours rather than to lay off staff. How do you feel about this?

_____

_____

_____

2. Stem cell research is an important new field of research. Do you think that the government should pay for this line of study?

_____

_____

_____

3. Women should stop smoking cigarettes during pregnancy. How would you convince a woman to do so?

_____

_____

_____

4. Do you think that state hospitals should be required to provide indigent health services free of charge?

_____

_____

_____

5. Deciding whether to work in a hospital or for a private doctor's practice is a decision that medical assistants make before graduation. In your opinion, which is better?

_____

_____

_____

AutoCAD

1. The machines that you and your team have used for drawing are outdated. You need to write a proposal for updated machines. What will you say to convince the managers to invest in new computers?

_____

_____

_____

2. In designing the house addition, you discover that it will cost more money than your original estimate. Write your first sentence of the new estimate to persuade the customer that the added costs are necessary.

_____

_____

_____

3. Following a long night of debate, you have not finished the drawings for the project. What will you tell your supervisor to convince her that more time is needed to complete the work?

_____

_____

_____

4. A recruiter from a rival company offers you a slightly higher salary. You want to continue working for your current employer and decide to write a proposal for a raise. What will you write for your opening sentence?

_____

_____

_____

5. Three companies in town will bid on the same design project as you. How will you persuade the customer to hire your company?

_____

_____

_____

Automotive Technology

1. A customer does not want to replace a worn timing belt even though you believe that continued driving is dangerous. What would you say to convince the customer of the danger?

_____

_____

_____

2. Your shop manager asks you to replace a broken transmission with a used one. While doing the repairs, you notice some problems with the used transmission. Convince your manager that this transmission will not work.

_____

_____

_____

3. You hear that the new dealership down the street is hiring mechanics and you are interested. What will you say to the repair manager when you deliver your resume?

_____

_____

_____

4. You and your friend have saved enough money to open your own garage. In order to borrow the rest of the money, you need to write a business proposal for the loan officer at the bank. How will you begin your proposal?

_____

_____

_____

5. Gasoline prices continue to rise steadily. More people are purchasing hybrid cars. Do you believe that this is an effective solution to the high gas price issue?

_____

_____

_____

Criminal Justice

1. Due to the state budget cuts, a third of the state's juvenile probation officers received lay off notices today. Persuade a friend that this layoff is or is not a good idea.

_____

_____

_____

2. As a supervising officer, you are concerned that your officers' cars are the oldest in the city's fleet. You write a proposal asking for new vehicles. Write a convincing first sentence to your proposal.

_____

_____

_____

3. Local ATF Officers warn of illegal trade activity in the area. How would you propose to catch the importers?

_____

_____

_____

4. Due to the lack of space in county jails, judges are releasing people who have been arrested for minor drug crimes. Do you agree or disagree with this solution?

_____

_____

_____

5. Outdoor surveillance cameras record activity downtown. There are at least ten mounted to street lights. Some townspeople complain that this is an infringement on their right to privacy. Convince them that the cameras are an effective means of crime prevention.

_____

_____

_____

Electronics

1. During the morning meeting, the manager told supervisors that some of the teams will hire two more electricians. Write the first sentence of your proposal to add two more members to your team.

_____

_____

_____

2. The storm destroyed the main transformer behind the building. To power the rest of the buildings, you recommend the installation of a new transformer. What will you write in your estimate to convince the owners to do this?

_____

_____

_____

3. You install a ceiling fan for a customer and discover that there is water in the wiring. The customer does not believe that this is a problem. Convince him that this is a dangerous situation.

_____

_____

_____

4. A friend asks advice about selecting a circuit board for his computer. You feel that he ought to keep the one that he has because it is compatible with the rest of the components. How will you convince him to keep it?

_____

_____

_____

5. You bid on a project to wire an apartment complex. To win the bid, you have to offer to complete the job for the least amount of money possible. Write your opening sentence to convince the possible customer to choose you even if you are not the lowest bidder.

_____

_____

_____

Information Technology

1. Many companies use spyware to detect programs that try to invade hard drives. Do you think that all computers should use spyware and firewalls as the best means for security?

_____

_____

_____

2. The server at work can no longer handle the computers attached to it. You need to write a proposal asking for funds to purchase a second server. How will you begin your proposal?

_____

_____

_____

3. You have bid on a job to set up three computer labs for the local high school. You will be offered the work if you are able to convince the principal of your ability to complete the job efficiently. Write the first sentence of your proposal.

_____

_____

_____

4. You will be late completing an animation project. To ask for more time, you must persuade your supervisor that the extra time is essential. How will you convince her to extend the deadline?

_____

_____

_____

5. Websites often interact with information on personal hard drives through cookies. Write a persuasive sentence convincing the reader that cookies are necessary.

_____

_____

_____

Paralegal Studies

1. For high profile cases, some lawyers hire psychologists to make recommendations for jury selection. Write a persuasive opening statement in support of this practice.

_____

_____

_____

2. Your law firm is expanding and you have applied for a promotion. What will you write to convince the partners that you are worthy of the promotion?

_____

_____

_____

3. One of the benefits of working for your law firm is that they reimburse law school classes with prior approval. How will you persuade them to pay for your law school classes?

_____

_____

_____

4. Even after working all night, you realize that you will not be able to complete the paper due in your torte class. How will you convince your professor to grant an extension to the deadline?

_____

_____

_____

5. You spend your weekends volunteering to work for a community legal assistance center. The funding for this project must be renewed in order to continue to be able to serve the community. What will the first sentence of your continued funding proposal say?

_____

_____

_____

⤜ *EXERCISE 4.3* ⤛

Rewrite each sentence from the given point of view to the opposite point of view. Write the words to reflect the statement and your position. For example,

Original Sentence: **I believe earning a college degree is a waste of time and money because many people are able to succeed in their careers without one.**

Rewritten Sentence: **I believe that earning a college degree is one of those most valuable investments that one can make towards the future; studying taught me to think more clearly and to broaden my view of life.**

Allied Health

1. I think that using universal precautions is pointless since so few patients are infected with life threatening viruses.

_____

_____

2. To me, hospitals should not allow nurses, surgical technicians, and medical assistants to work more than eight-hour shifts.

_____

_____

3. I believe that HIPAA regulations are not necessary; no one is interested in someone else's medical records.

_____

_____

AutoCAD

1. Copyright laws do not allow us to mimic someone else's character; it interferes with the creative process.

_____

_____

2. The plans for the sundeck are not practical because they do not take into account the trees close to the house in the back.

_____

_____

3. To resolve the flaw in the chimney design, I believe that it can be fixed using projection since that will show whether the chimney and the roof are attached properly.

_____

_____

Automotive Technology

1. The customer wants to add expensive rims to his car; this is a bad idea because the ones that he wants do not fit the wheels properly.

_____

_____

2. I warned Mike against buying used parts for his car in a junkyard because the parts are not guaranteed to work.

_____

_____

3. Oil needs to be changed every 3,000 miles no matter how new the car because of the possible wear on the engine.

_____

_____

Criminal Justice

1. The best way to control our country's drug problem is to keep all drug offenders in jail since they are the ones that continue the drug trade.

_____

_____

2. At the police academy, it is necessary for women and men to take different physical performance tests since women are weaker than men.

_____

_____

3. It is a waste to spend money on hiring more border patrol officers because they are not able to stop people from sneaking into our country.

_____

_____

Electronics

1. In the storm, it is important to send out as many road teams as possible to restore power even if the winds are strong because it is more dangerous to be without electricity.

_____

_____

2. It is better to work as a contractor than it is to work for someone else because you will earn more money.

_____

_____

3. Wires do not need to be enclosed in a conduit because the current carried by only a few of them is not dangerous.

_____

_____

Information Technology

1. School computer labs should be equipped with multimedia computers so that students have more options available for conducting research.

_____

_____

2. When purchasing a computer, be sure that it has a floppy drive installed because so many people still use this for primary data storage.

_____

_____

3. The safest option to connect everyone in the company is to create an intranet system because this will protect the company information from unauthorized access.

_____

_____

Paralegal Studies

1. Husband/wife privilege interferes with the ability for a fair trial; I think that if the spouse has pertinent knowledge that could affect the outcome of the case, he/she should testify.

_____

_____

2. Legal assistants, in some states, mediate divorce dissolution hearings which is not a good idea because attorneys are better trained.

_____

_____

3. Real estate is the most lucrative form of law for a legal assistant to enter because of the rise in real estate sales.

_____

_____

❧ *EXERCISE 4.4* ❧

For each example, write a paragraph in persuasive style using the given facts. Pay careful attention to your topic and conclusive sentences. Remember to state the facts and your opinion clearly. Use only words that support your point of view. For example,

> <u>Facts:</u> **In two months, you are graduating from college and decide to apply for a job as a legal assistant. To do this, you must write a persuasive cover letter.**

> *Persuasive Paragraph from Facts:* **I am applying for the posted position of Legal Assistant which I learned of through our attorney, Mr. Blackwell. In two months, I am graduating from City University with an Associate's degree in Paralegal Studies. While attending classes, I worked for this law firm as a legal secretary which challenged me to use my lessons from college to assist legal assistants and attorneys. My education, coupled with my experience with this law firm, can be a valuable asset to our clients and attorneys since I am already familiar with our office system of data collection and analysis.**

1. Facts: A young woman is excited to discover that she is pregnant. She believes that she does not need to see a doctor until the birth. Pretend that you are writing an article to persuade women that continuous medical attention is necessary.

   _____

   _____

   _____

   _____

   _____

   _____

   _____

2. Facts: The EMT was excited to learn that someone from his emergency team is to be assigned to work with the city's professional football team. He tries to convince his supervisor that he is the best person for the assignment.

   _____

   _____

   _____

   _____

   _____

   _____

   _____

3. Facts: The medical receptionist dreams of one day working as a pharmacy technologist; her studies conclude in the fall. She wants to persuade her doctor to write a letter of recommendation for her for her job search.

   _____

   _____

   _____

   _____

   _____

   _____

   _____

4. Facts: A patient is terrified of entering the MRI machine. He is claustrophobic. Convince him that this is a necessary procedure.

_____

_____

_____

_____

_____

_____

_____

5. Facts: The surgical technologist finished working a 12-hour shift when he was asked to work another four hours. What can he say to convince his supervisor that he cannot work an additional half shift?

_____

_____

_____

_____

_____

_____

_____

AutoCAD

1. Facts: Sheila will interview for an apprentice position in a jewelry design shop tomorrow. What can she say to convince the interviewer that she is the best person for the apprenticeship?

_____

_____

_____

_____

_____

_____

2. Facts: He worries about career prospects in mechanical design; it depends too closely on the economy. Three of his friends were recently laid off from their jobs. He decides to write a proposal to expand business in his department. What can he write to support his expansion idea?

_____

_____

_____

_____

_____

_____

_____

3. Facts: When Marc graduates from college, he wants to work as a landscape architect contractor. What should the first paragraph of his cover letter say to convince a prospective employer to read his resume?

_____

_____

_____

_____

_____

_____

_____

4. Facts: I am practicing adapting my two-dimensional designs into three-dimensional ones. I asked my instructor to help me this afternoon. He said he is too busy. How do I convince him that I need assistance in order to complete the project?

_____

_____

_____

_____

_____

_____

_____

5. Facts: The student anticipates that the class topic is to learn how to form solid models from wireframe drawings. His friend does not want to attend class. What will the student say to change his friend's mind?

_____

_____

_____

_____

_____

_____

_____

Automotive Technology

1. Facts: Learning to drive a manual, Lisa fails to shift properly. She strips the gears and does not seem to care. What will you tell her to show her the danger of moving gears without pushing in the clutch first?

_____

_____

_____

_____

_____

_____

_____

2. Facts: It is important to change the oil in your car every 3,000 miles. If not, the engine wears down. How can you convince a customer of the importance of this?

_____

_____

_____

_____

_____

_____

_____

3. Facts: The mechanic is too excited to sleep; he starts his first job in a dealership tomorrow. He is meeting with the shop manager early in the morning to discuss his salary. What can he say to persuade the manager to pay him more than the posted salary?

_____

_____

_____

_____

_____

_____

4. Facts: Ernesto spent all night assembling a four-cylinder engine in preparation for his test in the morning. He is not sure that he will be able to finish by morning. What can he write in his email to the customer to convince him to allow him more time for completion?

_____

_____

_____

_____

_____

_____

5. Facts: To help a customer, you call four junkyards in search of a used transmission. You have not been able to find one and are uncertain of whom else to call. In order to complete the job, you must persuade your supervisor to charge less money for labor.

_____

_____

_____

_____

_____

_____

Criminal Justice

1. Facts: As an officer, you and your partner respond to a domestic violence call on the corner of 39th and Elm. You hear shouting as you approach the house. What will you say to persuade the couple to come outside of the house?

    _____

    _____

    _____

    _____

    _____

    _____

    _____

2. Facts: An animal cruelty investigator is called to a house where there are 20 cages of neglected dogs. The dogs need medical assistance. There is not enough shelter space for the animals, so you need to convince another shelter to house some of the dogs. Write a paragraph telling how you will do this.

    _____

    _____

    _____

    _____

    _____

    _____

    _____

3. Facts: Upon release from the halfway house, a 14-year-old juvenile thanks his counselor for supporting him. What can the counselor do to influence the youth to attend school and to stay away from trouble?

    _____

    _____

    _____

    _____

    _____

    _____

    _____

4. Facts: A criminal justice student spends the day shadowing a probation officer. She decides that she would like to pursue a career in probation based upon this experience. To gain more experience, she proposes that she work as an intern in the probation office. What will she write in her proposal?

_____

_____

_____

_____

_____

_____

5. Facts: Following a plane crash, a K-9 unit joins the search for bodies. There are many survivors who need help. Volunteers are needed for this task. The publicity officer from the local precinct pleads for community members to volunteer to assist. What would the first paragraph of the press release say?

_____

_____

_____

_____

_____

_____

Electronics

1. Facts: The outside lights are not working because water seeped into the wire casing. All wires need to be replaced. Convince the homeowner that this is a danger if left for too long.

_____

_____

_____

_____

_____

_____

2. Facts: A computer technician from the ACE company calls to hire you to install the wires for the new automated phone system. You need to charge more money than he estimated for the job. How will you justify your raised estimate?

_____

_____

_____

_____

_____

_____

3. Facts: You arrive at class to discover that there is a test, but you did not study the calculations for Ohm's law theory. Convince your instructor to allow you to take the test later in the week.

_____

_____

_____

_____

_____

_____

4. Facts: You decide to work as a line installer because you can use electronics training and work outside. There are advertised jobs with the local electric company. Write the first paragraph of your cover letter convincing the employer to consider you for the position.

_____

_____

_____

_____

_____

_____

5. Facts: While working on a construction site, you overhear that another electrician is to wire the other buildings in the complex for more money than you charge. Convince the foreman that you can complete the job better and cheaper than the other electrician can.

_____

_____

_____

_____

_____

_____

_____

Information Technology

1. Facts: Feeling deflated, Juan left class upset that COBOL is not used in business programming any longer because it is the language that he knows best. Juan wants to complete his class assignment in COBOL; how will he propose this to his instructor?

_____

_____

_____

_____

_____

_____

_____

2. Facts: The systems administrator is convinced that the random error messages indicate software incompatibility. She advised that the customer download a patch. The customer does not believe the administrator. What will she say to persuade the customer to download the patch?

_____

_____

_____

_____

_____

_____

_____

3. Facts: The customer purchased a printer, but the salesman is trying to convince him to purchase extra printer cartridges as well. What can the salesman say to persuade the customer to do this?

_____

_____

_____

_____

_____

_____

_____

4. Facts: Thomas needs to purchase a new computer. He seeks your advice. Which computer do you recommend and why?

_____

_____

_____

_____

_____

_____

_____

5. Facts: When Mary Ann graduates, she wants to work in an MIS department. In order to apply, what will she write in the first paragraph of her cover letter to convince the employer that she is a viable candidate?

_____

_____

_____

_____

_____

_____

_____

Paralegal Studies

1. Facts: A paralegal student spends a day shadowing a legal assistant in a large law firm. The pace of the office is frenzied. This experience excites the student so much that she wants to work as an intern in that office. What will the student write in her internship proposal to convince the partners to accept her as an intern?

_____

_____

_____

_____

_____

_____

_____

2. Facts: A woman who works in a travel service office accessed client flights in order to steal their frequent flyer miles. She diverted the miles into a dummy account. You are assisting the defendant's lawyer. What will the attorney say in his opening statement to show the woman's guilt?

_____

_____

_____

_____

_____

_____

_____

3. Facts: To prepare for voir dire, the attorney scheduled the legal assistants to work overtime. You are to leave on a cruise in the morning. How will you convince your boss to let you to take this trip rather than work on this case?

_____

_____

_____

_____

_____

_____

_____

4. Facts: A couple comes to the legal clinic because they are experiencing severe financial problems. You must help them decide between filing Chapter 7 or Chapter 13. You suggest that they file Chapter 13; what will you say to influence their decision?

_____

_____

_____

_____

_____

_____

_____

5. Facts: You need to research two projects, but you feel behind. What will you say to the other assistants in your office to persuade them to help you?

_____

_____

_____

_____

_____

_____

_____

The challenge in writing a persuasive essay is to reflect a clear perspective throughout the piece. It is important to choose your point of view before you begin to write. In your outline, write the topic sentence, then list specific supporting details. Outlining will help you to organize your thoughts in a manner that will sound convincing to your reader. Write a paragraph using a topic of your choice. Be sure that you select an issue that has two or more clear perspectives and that you feel passionate about the topic.

Argumentative Writing

TIPS

Definition

The purpose of argumentative writing is not to create conflict between writer and reader. It is, instead, to make the reader aware of your point of view. Arguments exist to persuade others to alter their position regarding a topic. So, to persuade the reader to re-evaluate his opinion, the writer must create compelling reasons for the reader to move from one position to another.

Career Uses

Use the argumentative style when writing a proposal for change in policy or resource use. Managers utilize this style when refuting customer service claims or when writing responses to complaints. Career specific journals and newsletters use argumentative writing to present ideas and to invite reader response.

Principles of Argumentative Writing

How do you know when to use argumentative writing? Look for these types of questions or prompts:

- *Any question that directly or indirectly asks "should" such as, "Should medical assistants be required to work twelve-hour shifts instead of eight-hour shifts?"*

- *Any question that asks the writer to agree or disagree.*

To effectively write an argumentative essay, begin with the opening proposition that clearly states your position. Follow it with background information to support the position. Use supporting details to connect your argument with your audience. Strengthen the argument through a summarization of opposing views and close with a restatement of your position. The key to writing a strong argumentative essay is to use strong transition words to move from one point to another.

Avoid these Common Mistakes

Here are some of the common mistakes made by writers when using argumentative style:

- *Do not base an idea or proposal on weak logic; we say that the writer has committed a logical fallacy.*

- *Failure to use transition words between ideas, thereby confusing the reader.*

- *Failure to capture the reader's attention to develop interest in the proposition.*

EXERCISES

⟨ *EXERCISE 4.6* ⟩

Complete the following sentences using words that strengthen the arguments. For example,

Original Sentence: **I firmly believe that in order for our company to grow, we**

_____.

Rewritten Sentence: **I firmly believe that in order for our company to grow, we must lay off a quarter of our staff to save on overhead.**

Allied Health

1. It is unfair to require medical assistants to work twelve-hour shifts because _____
    _____.

2. Staff nurses earn less money per shift than pool nurses do. I believe that this is wrong
    because_____
    _____.

3. When the new wing of the clinic opens, patients who cannot pay for services will not be
    treated. This wrong in my opinion _____
    _____.

4. Hospital policy states that all medical personnel must attend training in HIPAA annually;
    I think that this is a waste of time since _____
    _____.

5. In our office, senior staff members are promoted over junior ones despite qualifications. I
    do not think that this is fair because_____
    _____.

AutoCAD

1. To save money, most of the studio's animators should be fired because _____
    _____.

2. Company policy dictates that all engineers must use their computers when working on
    client designs. This policy is a bad one because _____
    _____.

3. In my opinion, the AutoCAD program at our school is one of the best due to _____
_____.

4. Though the team opted to use a foggy background setting for the storyboard, I disagreed
because_____
_____.

5. Our proposal to update the computer system was denied because there is not enough
money in the budget to support the proposed upgrades, but this is a short sighted decision
due to _____
_____.

Automotive Technology

1. Even though car manufacturers suggest an engine oil change every 5,000 miles, it is
better to change it every 3,000 because _____
_____.

2. Some new cars include DVD players below the rearview mirror, but this is a dangerous
trend _____
_____.

3. The new policy of preventing customers from watching the mechanic work on their cars
is wrong _____
_____.

4. The practice of replacing worn parts with used parts is not always a good one because
_____
_____.

5. Some shops hire mechanics that have not passed their certification tests, but this practice
is still a practical one since _____
_____.

Criminal Justice

1. Capitol punishment is necessary as a deterrent to crime because _____
_____.

2. To reduce cruelty to animals, penalties must _____
_____.

3. I believe that all juveniles who commit crimes should _____

    _____

4. Impounded vehicles should be sold at auctions _____

    _____.

5. All those convicted of drug charges should serve strict jail sentences because _____

    _____.

Electronics

1. To generate more energy, wind power should be harnessed rather than building more
    nuclear plants_____

    _____.

2. Tree limbs should be cut away from power lines before the arrival of the storm season

    _____

    _____.

3. Everyone should take advantage of energy conservation programs offered by electric
    companies because _____

    _____.

4. All linemen should be required to attend safety procedures training annually _____

    _____.

5. In my opinion, our electronics program at school is one of the best because _____

    _____.

Information Technology

1. I believe that we should invest in the most expensive server that we can afford because

    _____

    _____.

2. Some software companies monopolize the market using unfair tactics; to me, this is
    wrong _____

    _____.

3. Websites that allow people to exchange music files are _____

    _____.

4. Computer hackers who break into a system with a non-malicious virus must be_____

    _____

    _____.

5. In my opinion, our Information Technology program at school is better than yours because _____

_____.

Paralegal Studies

1. I disagree with our firm's policy of requiring legal assistants to work overtime during certain times of the year because _____

_____.

2. According to our state law, legal assistants can perform only some duties without supervision of a lawyer. They should be allowed to do more _____

_____

_____.

3. I believe that capitol punishment does not deter people from committing crimes _____

_____

_____.

4. Illegal immigrants who have resided in the United States for a period of five years _____ shouldbe given legal status because _____

_____.

5. The Paralegal Studies program at our school is better than at yours because _____

_____

_____.

❧ EXERCISE 4.7 ❧

Below are some examples of opening argumentative statements. Remember that one of the features of writing effective arguments is to recognize and mention other positions than the one you support. For this reason, write a sentence that opposes the given ones. For example,

Original Sentence: To decrease crime in the neighborhood, the local police chief needs to assign more officers to the area because an increased presence will deter crime.

Rewritten Sentence: An increase in police presence in our neighborhood will cause an increase in crime; this is because criminals will conduct business behind closed doors making their activities harder to monitor.

Allied Health

1. Quality of patient care depends on the patient's ability to pay for service because health insurance companies authorize procedures.

    _____

    _____

2. Dental hygienists should be allowed to practice separately from dentists since they must demonstrate capability in specific skill areas in order to earn their licenses.

    _____

    _____

3. It is not necessary to wear gloves when treating a patient who claims to be healthy because they will not pass communicable diseases.

    _____

    _____

AutoCAD

1. It is acceptable to use someone else's designs if a client is willing to pay for the work.

    _____

    _____

2. Each minute used in drawing drafts should not be billed, instead, a flat fee should be charged.

    _____

    _____

3. Since the room that is to be added to the house cannot be built on the east side of the house because it will not be aesthetically pleasing, we must convince the client to change his mind.

    _____

    _____

Automotive

1. Cars should be powered with ethanol so that we can preserve our petroleum supplies.

    _____

    _____

2. The motto that "customers are always correct" is a poor one since not all customers understand the needs of their cars and therefore, neglect important work.

_____

_____

3. Mechanics should stop to help motorists who have broken down on the highway.

_____

_____

Criminal Justice

1. All rookie officers should work on the night shift during their first year with the force because there are less disturbances during that time.

_____

_____

2. Criminal Justice majors who want to work as probation officers should be required to work as interns first so that they can develop practical skills.

_____

_____

3. To apply to work with the Central Intelligence Agency, one must undergo a number of tests. I believe that these tests are excessive and simply allow them to eliminate whomever they like illegally.

_____

_____

Electronics

1. All electronics students should pass an internship before being allowed to graduate so that they can practice their skills.

_____

_____

2. There is no need for electricians to pass a licensing exam because the state only created licensing as another means to raise revenue.

_____

_____

3. It is necessary to place large electric poles in neighborhoods to ensure proper delivery of power.

_____

_____

Information Technology

1. When programmers add adware programs that record and report consumer browsing behavior, it is harmless to the consumer and beneficial to the company.

_____

_____

2. Many companies install software to monitor employee email without telling them that it exists, but by doing so, the company is violating the employees' privacy.

_____

_____

3. In my opinion, all computers should be sold with antispyware to guard against the most common malicious viruses that are unleashed across the Internet.

_____

_____

Paralegal Studies

1. Laws that allow citizens in some states to vote early are illegal because the polling places are not properly regulated, allowing for possible fraud.

_____

_____

2. In my opinion, laws that protect husbands and wives from testifying against each other should be changed because their communications are not classified as privileged in the constitution.

_____

_____

3. I believe that the practice of billing clients by the hour is unethical because they are often charged for more work than was actually completed.

_____

_____

❈ EXERCISE 4.8 ❖

For this exercise, write a letter to the editor in response to an article that appeared in last week's paper. To write a strong argument, state your position, support it using specific details and examples, mention possible other positions on the subject and then conclude with a summary of your argument.

Allied Health

In last Sunday's paper, you read that a stem cell research laboratory will open in the hospital where you work. People protest outside of the hospital each day; you feel strongly about the value of this research (either agree or disagree that it is valuable). Write a letter to the editor expressing your position.

_____

_____

_____

_____

_____

_____

_____

_____

_____

_____

_____

_____

_____

_____

_____

_____

_____

AutoCAD

In last Sunday's paper, you read an article stating that many draft designs, created using AutoCAD programs, are being duplicated by architects. As computer design programs become more sophisticated, it is easier to use someone else's designs without his permission. Write a letter to the editor expressing your position about copying other designs. (Do you believe that it is wrong to duplicate another's design without his permission or not?)

_____

_____

_____

_____

_____

_____

_____

_____

_____

_____

_____

_____

_____

_____

Automotive

In last Sunday's paper, you read that many new car designers are cutting costs by using plastic parts in the engine. As a mechanic, you have already worked with cars that have these parts. Write a letter to the editor expressing your opinion about whether you believe that this is a good practice or not.

_____

_____

_____

_____

_____

_____

_____

_____

_____

Criminal Justice

In last Sunday's paper, you read an interview with your local state representative; she is supporting a bill designed to punish drug crimes with longer jail sentences. According to her, the enactment of tougher penalties will reduce the number of people who are arrested for using or selling drugs. Write a letter to the editor expressing your support or distaste for the bill.

_____

Electronics

In last Sunday's paper, you read that the local electric company plans to build large electric poles through your neighborhood in order to make power delivery more efficient. Many of your neighbors registered their complaints and support in the article. You also feel strongly about this issue. Write a letter to the editor expressing your support or opposition to the addition of these poles.

_____

_____

_____

_____

_____

_____

_____

_____

_____

_____

_____

_____

_____

Information Technology

In last Sunday's paper, you read an article written by a local college professor discussing the pros and cons of Internet security. You work for a company that writes security programs for businesses. In the article, the professor states that he believes that security programs are useless because there is always someone who is able to find access to a business' server. Write a letter to the editor expressing your agreement or disagreement with the writer's opinion.

_____

_____

_____

_____

_____

_____

_____

_____

_____

_____

_____

_____

_____

Paralegal Studies

In last Sunday's paper, you read that a local group of law professionals plan to start a private, non-profit legal clinic for people who cannot afford to pay for legal counsel. This clinic is to be staffed by volunteer lawyers, legal assistants and legal secretaries. Some law professionals are opposed to this because they believe that this will detract from their business. Write a letter to the editor expressing either your support of or opposition to the establishment of the clinic.

_____
_____
_____
_____
_____
_____
_____
_____
_____
_____
_____
_____
_____
_____

REVIEW OF THE NINE WRITING STYLES

**Now that you have practiced recognizing and writing different writing styles, see if you can identify each writing style in the following paragraphs. Once you have identified the style, write down a reason for your choice.**

1. Never in my life have I worked so hard to complete a project! Our supervisor called me at home around 2:30 A.M. and asked me to report to the office immediately because the bottom two floors of our building flooded. When I arrived on the scene, two trucks filled with damaged computers pulled out of the parking lot. I entered the building wading through the blanket of water that still covered the floor. "Grab the equipment from that corner of the office and take it to the truck waiting outsid," barked my supervisor. From that moment, I carried and loaded equipment and mopped floors for ten hours without break.

This is an example of _____ writing.

Some characteristics of this type of writing are:

_____

_____

_____

_____

_____

2. There are many types of medical careers available. The key to choosing the best one for you is to research each one. For example, if you plan to earn an Associate's degree, you might study to work as a surgical technologist, dental hygienist, medical assistant, or pharmacy technician. If you plan to earn a Bachelor's degree, you might enroll in a nursing program. If you are interested in earning a graduate degree in medicine, you might take classes to become a doctor, dentist, or nurse practitioner. Whichever you decide, the key to your success will be your ability to study.

This is an example of _____ writing.

Some characteristics of this type of writing are:

_____

_____

_____

_____

_____

3. Juveniles who are arrested for drug possession should not be locked in detention centers; these youth need treatment, not incarceration. Studies conducted by the National Office for Drug Control indicate that juveniles who engage in a drug treatment program within a month of arrest show high recovery rates. Those that spend time incarcerated without treatment show the highest rates of recidivism. For this reason, states need to allocate more money for youth drug prevention and treatment programs. This is the only hope that we, as a society, have for helping our children to live better lives.

This is an example of _____ writing.

Some characteristics of this type of writing are:

_____

_____

_____

_____

_____

4. Mr. Johnson called early this morning, angry that his house would be foreclosed upon in a week. I checked the financial records supplied by the bank, and according to them, Mr. Johnson has not paid his mortgage for three months. In fact, there were three prior months of late payments. It was a difficult conversation with Mr. Johnson as I attempted to convince him that if he is unable to make house payments he will have to move. Even though I knew that legally, there is nothing that can be done, I referred him to speak with one of our attorneys.

This is an example of _____ writing.

Some characteristics of this type of writing are:

_____

_____

_____

_____

_____

5. I am trying to decide what I should do once I graduate from school with my Associate's degree in electronics. My friend suggested that I work as an electrical contractor so that I can choose the jobs that are best suited to my skills. Then, one of my instructors offered to get me an interview with a friend of his. There are advantages and disadvantages to both choices. Working for myself would allow me to arrange my activities according to my desires while working for someone else will not. However, if I work for a company, I will be guaranteed work; that guarantee does not exist if I contract. This decision will require much thought.

This is an example of _____ writing.

Some characteristics of this type of writing are:

_____

_____

_____

_____

_____

6. Mrs. Kaflooey reported that she had a temperature of 102 degrees for three days prior to coming to the emergency room. Patient's blood pressure is in the normal range. Patient's heartbeat has elevated between the first and second check. In addition, patient's skin appears clammy and pale. Due to her worsening condition, I requested that the doctor see her immediately.

This is an example of _____ writing.

Some characteristics of this type of writing are:

_____

_____

_____

_____

_____

7. "That's it! I am tired of our arguing the point. We have carefully drawn and revised each of our characters. If the client is displeased with the final draft, then ask him to supply specific criticisms or suggestions so that we can have a constructive conversation about this. Each time that we met with him, he indicated that he loved the concept. What has changed? Darn it, we have worked too hard and too long to have to begin this again."

This is an example of _____ writing.

Some characteristics of this type of writing are:

_____

_____

_____

_____

_____

8. From a distance, I could see that the truck leaned to one side. It did not appear as if it was rolling on a flat tire and I did not see any smoke emanating from the back. I could not diagnose the problem yet. Once it turned into our garage, I could see that the truck had a broken wheel axle. The sound was excruciating as metal scraped against metal, emitting a pitched squeal. Frantically, I begged the driver to stop and get out of the truck.

This is an example of _____ writing.

Some characteristics of this type of writing are:

_____

_____

_____

_____

_____

9. Before you begin your job search, write a cover letter, a resume, and a list of preferred jobs. Once you assemble these, call your friends and family members to notify them of your search. Ask if anyone knows someone who works in your field. If so, contact this person and ask if you can meet with him/her to ask some questions about the field. Take notes and thank this person. Now that you have conducted some research and have made some contacts, begin to look for your dream job!

This is an example of _____ writing.

Some characteristics of this type of writing are:

_____

_____

_____

_____

_____

Part III
Punctuation

Chapter 5
Simple Punctuation

Commas

⤜ *EXERCISE 5.1* ⤛

In each of the sentences below, add a comma in the appropriate place. Remember that the purpose of the comma is to separate similar and dissimilar items and people from each other.

1. The client's attorney the client the defendant's attorney and the defendant met in a room at the courthouse to file a deposition.

2. To assist the client the legal assistant prepared questions to be used during the deposition.

3. The medical insurance claim information is to be sent to 2635 Westerly Ave. Memphis Tennessee by tomorrow morning.

4. Shelia Marty and Thomas need to select backgrounds and wipes to complete their animation project.

5. With circuits overloaded the team of electricians worked to create an alternate wiring plan.

6. Yesterday the managers met with the technology committee to discuss the timeline the system upgrades the allocation of funds and possible locations for the new server.

7. The manager John Dorsey will start work in the garage this morning.

8. His work in the operating room is a meticulous efficient example for all medical students to follow.

9. "From this draft you are to create a 3-D rendering so that we can begin production in a few days" the supervisor directed.

10. Mechanics learn how to diagnose fix and perform preventive maintenance on engines while training to take the certification test sponsored by the National Institute for Automotive Service Excellence.

11. After we will use the resistor to test the voltage given by the motor.

12. The probation officer stated "I met with the probationer on Monday morning before noon for his scheduled appointment. We scheduled another appointment for the same time next month."

13. However the licensing agreement reads that the program can be installed on three separate home computers.

14. No such law has been enacted in the past two hundred years and yet it is unclear as to why.

15. Ms. Dartmouth the medical assistant is not able to cover the third shift tonight.

16. In this drawing you need to take information from a three-dimensional perspective and develop it into a 3view instead.

17. Therefore an open or break anywhere in the control circuit will prevent the operation of the starter motor.

18. Officer McHaley the officer on duty can answer your questions.

19. The advanced electronics exam is a long difficult test suitable for those who are close to graduating this semester.

20. Not all software written for that system is inefficient however.

21. Penal Law 1053 states that "Any person who while engaged in hunting shall discharge a firearm or operate a long bow in a culpably negligent manner is guilty of criminal negligence while engaged in hunting."

22. The doctor asked the nurse to take the medical history check the blood pressure and give a flu shot to the patient in room four.

23. Thus when the inductance is increased the opposition to current increases.

24. In this exercise we will practice scaling the text and lines that you completed drawing previously.

25. The store processor is a file server for the cash registers providing product and pricing information while capturing the customer's purchasing preferences.

26. Suppose for example that you are unable to find the references that you need in the law library then you can use this online database.

27. "I need my car fixed no later than 4:00 A.M. this afternoon because I have a meeting" implored the customer.

28. Fluorides can be given to patients topically through the water system and through vitamin supplements.

29. First create the image that you want to develop and then decide on the dimensions.

30. Jayne fast-talking and bright managed to elude police for years before being captured today.

31. The Eastshore electric company the new area utility provider will lower power rates for all customers.

32. Ms. Jackson directed "Place the new computers in the back of the room so that we can set up each one individually."

33. The width of the grooves the width of the lands between the ring grooves and the number of the rings are major factors in determining minimum piston height.

34. Tomorrow I graduate with my Associate's degree in electronic technology.

35. Dr. Parker the new physician on staff will be giving a talk tomorrow for all medical assistants.

36. Talented hard-working students are hired by that firm every summer.

37. Vapor lock is caused by bubbles that form in the fuel preventing proper operation of the fuel pump carburetor or fuel-injection system.

38. The Internet computer networks business servers and automated data systems present many new opportunities for committing criminal activity.

39. "I believe that the heating element in the water heater needs replacing" she reported.

40. The problem is that in order to properly install run and test the antivirus software the entire system will be shut down for an hour.

41. This case exciting yet challenging is quite time consuming.

42. For absorption to occur the correct form of the drug must be given by the route intended.

43. The complex symbol is the completed fully detailed model.

44. To cause inflation the closing of the arming sensor is required to provide the power-side voltage to the inflator module.

45. "You need to stay seated until we come for you" the officer told the detainee.

46. Also the period can be measured from any peak in a given cycle to the corresponding peak in the next cycle.

47. DSL is always operational meaning that the channel is active at all times.

48. Since no contract exists the recipient is under no obligation to either pay the merchant or return the item.

49. "Sit back in the chair and close your eyes to relax while you wait for the dentist" the hygienist recommended.

50. The customer the man in the orange shirt sitting in the corner requested a word with the mechanic.

51. "Your performance this month was exceptional" his supervisor reported.

52. The secondary winding is connected to the circuit containing the rectifier filter terminal and regulator.

53. The new laptops slimmer and quicker than the older models will revolutionize our industry.

54. The case files the ones that you requested are sitting in the warehouse waiting for delivery.

55. Yesterday I discovered that the local pharmacy has openings for full-time technicians.

56. "I met with the customer an hour ago" I began before being interrupted by the ringing of the phone.

57. There is also the danger of freezing when a battery is discharged because the electrolyte is mostly water.

58. The agent the one that uncovered the smuggling ring was promoted this morning.

59. Five transport technologies are in widespread use including (1) frame delay (2) ATM (3) DSL (4) ISDN (5) SMDS.

60. Those expenses might include the difference between the contract price and the going rate of the open market lost profits replacement or completion costs or other amounts.

61. Writing new programs ones that increase line productivity is both time consuming and lucrative.

62. Next check the patient's cholesterol so that we have all of the necessary information to make the diagnosis.

63. The architect will meet you on Tuesday October 30 at 3:00 P.M.

64. "Check the oil gasket oil tray and oil level because the customer is worried that there may be a leak" Jake told the mechanic.

65. Correctional officers who are well-trained often work in dangerous conditions.

66. When two like poles are brought close together they repel each other.

67. Be sure that when you purchase your new computer that you also purchase cables a printer and system software.

68. A legal assistant is prohibited of course from rendering legal advice in either situation although the attendance of the paralegal at these events is not generally a problem.

69. Touch cuddling visual and auditory stimulation are all critical for the infant.

70. Keep in mind however that using too small a lens length can greatly distort the display of the model.

71. The mid-size car of the year the one that most consumers bought is the one that needs the least repairs.

72. Recently the city police attempted to disrupt gang activity by passing a city ordinance prohibiting public loitering in front of local businesses.

73. Please meet the other linemen on Wednesday June 1 at the regional office for the annual safety training.

74. The use of instant messages on the Internet a sort of combination of real-time chat and e-mail has grown rapidly since it was introduced in the late 1990s.

75. "Prepare the briefs according to the format discussed in class" the professor said as he gave the assignment.

76. When patients fail to floss they develop more cavities.

77. This method of drawing circles is almost the same as the radius method except you do not use the default and you will see that the rubber band works differently.

78. Resistors as well as other components should be operated substantially below their rated values to enhance their reliability.

79. The computer may therefore need to scan several hundred feet of tape to find the record you want.

80. Also one party may act as the primary custodial parent while both parties share parental responsibilities on issues such as religion schooling medical treatment and other matters.

81. "So your next appointment is scheduled for our new office located at 364 High Street behind the new strip mall" the receptionist informed the patient.

82. To use it you need to specify the present orientation of the object relative to the coordinate system.

83. This type of master cylinder is also called dual-diameter bore step-bore or fast-fill master cylinder.

84. In some cases after isolating a fault to a particular circuit it may be necessary to isolate the problem to a single component in the circuit.

85. The Small Business Administration a branch of the United States government was created to assist small-business owners.

86. Terrorism as a criminal activity and the prevention of further acts of terrorism became primary concerns of the government following the attacks of September 11 2001.

87. When the contract offer was originally made the buyer gave the seller until 5:00 P.M. on May 16 2004 to accept.

88. Vitamin D which is largely derived from sunshine is instrumental in balancing the calcium and phosphorus ratio in the body.

89. The Shell suboption creates a hollow thin wall with a specified thickness.

90. Determine if there is a fault and if so identify it.

91. This idea stresses that in general IT works best when it adjusts to people not when people have to adjust to it.

92. "Have a seat the attorney will be with you in a moment" replied the receptionist to the client.

93. Appointment control will prevent overcrowding keep hours within desired limits organize the dentist's production time assign tasks to the proper individual and provide patients with definite appointment times.

94. The draft left on the table is the one that he needed for this morning's meeting.

95. Next check the circuit breaker usually located on the fuse panel using a test light.

96. The electrician is scheduled to check the system next week Thursday August 14 at 2:00 P.M.

97. The system upgrade is efficient fast and will save your technicians countless hours.

98. In light of the discussion it should be clear that depending on the legal issues involved he will be found innocent.

99. Medical assistants surgical technicians and nurses will attend the same orientation on Tuesday.

100. Sean boasted "What did the client think of our presentation yesterday? Our drawings were definitely the best there."

End Punctuation

⟨ EXERCISE 5.2 ⟩

For each of the sentences below, choose the appropriate end punctuation mark: period, question mark, or exclamation point. If you cannot decide, it is best to end with a period.

1. Late last night, the officer spotted three men breaking into the bank

2. What do you think is the best method for determining the value of the equivalent resistance of the input circuit

3. When the victim reported to the precinct, he was still in shock from witnessing the murder

4. Beware of the sasser worm; it will destroy your hard drive

5. Walking home from work, it occurred to me that I left the deposition papers on my desk; could you bring them with you when you come

6. What do you mean that Jane quit We have to replace her immediately

7. Working late at night can be hazardous to your health

8. Use caution when connecting jumper cables to battery terminals on a car; they might explode if the connection is wrong

9. Do you know when they are going to add more dental hygienists to the staff

10. The client liked our drawings That is the best news that I have heard in ages

11. Call 9-1-1, a lineman has been struck by lightening

12. To ensure proper care, bathe the wound twice daily and replace the dressing

13. Do we want to use a wireframe or surface model with these drafts

14. How he conducts his operating room is strictly his choice

15. Route the wires over the door so that no one will trip on the cables

16. Many feel that the law is unconstitutional; what are your feelings about it

17. Given the treatment options, she is afraid of choosing the wrong one

18. I need help right away My car broke down on a remote highway

19. Which do you prefer: to serve five years of probation or one year in jail

20. We are planning a career fair for next week Are you interested in participating

Apostrophes

⚡ *EXERCISE 5.3* ⚡

Add an apostrophe to each of these sentences. Some require more than one apostrophe, so read each sentence carefully.

1. While in the operating room, the surgical technologist couldnt answer her phone.

2. Yesterday, the engineer completed his plans for the project and now hes waiting for approval from the client to begin construction.

3. Did you try to loosen the lug nuts because the customer said that he wasnt able to get them to budge?

4. He left his tools at the last customers house; hell have to return to retrieve them.

5. To create the clients webpage, the web designer asked for a meeting with the design team to gather their opinions.

6. Are you sure shes willing to participate in the research study? Let me know if she wont.

7. After everyone left last night, I wasnt able to concentrate on the research for the case, so I left for home instead.

8. Does anyone know its origin? I am certain that I shouldve known that.

9. Sometimes, its stressful to work in our office especially during the flu season when we cant see everyone who walks into the clinic.

10. I didnt understand yesterdays lesson about creating chamfers and fillets on solid objects though I stayed up all night trying.

11. Ive discovered that if I start the engine without pumping the gas, the motor seems sluggish; can you please take a look at it?

12. He wasnt able to check the resistance because the coil isnt large enough.

13. Like stress, fatigue can affect a police officers performance.

14. The computer users desktop is not working properly; its not showing all of the startup icons.

15. Wouldnt it better if you considered filing a claim against him?

16. For now, Im considering working as a per diem home health care worker instead of working full time for one home. What do you think about that?

17. The belts squealing indicates a problem that should be addressed immediately.

18. I left a copy of my resume and a cover letter with him yesterday even though he said that theyre not hiring anyone presently.

19. The images lines seem rough to me, arent you able to smooth them?

20. Shes going to intern in the fall with the department though she cant spend a full day with the officer. Shell still earn her required hours.

Chapter 6
Advanced Punctuation

Semicolons

Semicolons can be used in two ways: to connect directly related independent sentences and to separate items in a list (dates, cities and states, for example) which contain internal commas.

EXERCISE 6.1

Insert semicolons in the appropriate places.

1. Various kinds of permissible activities require the paralegal to use legal judgment as long as the attorney reviews and approves the documents prior to sending them, the attorney takes responsibility.
2. Many formulas exist for assessing reading levels of written material nurses involved in developing written health teaching materials should write for lower levels.
3. Basic to the conflict perspective is the belief that the conflict is a fundamental aspect of social life at best, according to this perspective, formal agencies of society control the unempowered to comply with the rules.
4. A starter solenoid is an electromagnetic switch containing two separate, but connected, electromagnetic windings this switch is used to engage the starter drive and control the current from the battery to the starter motor.
5. Digestion begins in the oral cavity the enzyme ptyalin begins the digestion of starch and lubricates the food bolus.
6. When inserting a 3D model, it is important to orient the model this orientation usually is controlled by the current model's presently active UCS working plane.
7. When resistors are connected in the parallel, the current has more than one path the number of current paths is equal to the number of parallel branches.
8. The universal serial bus (USB) is one of the most recent additions to PC's it was created as a general-purpose port that can connect up to 128 devices, all using the samc connector.

9. Data communication is an integral component of information technology and many computing application records of text and data in a job database can include, for example, employee information including name, date hired, and job title as in this individual record Sally Thomas, August 2, 1988, Customer service representative Morgan Farris, May 4, 1991, Advertising director Bert Render, March 2 1976, Marketing manager and Earl James, February 5, 1982, Quality control supervisor.

10. The usefulness of Thevenin's theorem can be illustrated when it is applied to a Wheatstone bridge circuit for example consider the case when a load resistor is connected to the output terminals of a Wheatstone Bridge.

11. An interactive method for displaying a view of the model can be accomplished by using the 3DORBIT command you can access the command by typing it on the command line, picking it from the View pull-down menu, or using the 3D Orbit icon.

12. Congenital refers to a condition that exists at or before birth some common congenital defects of the oral cavity are missing teeth, cleft palate, and many facial defects.

13. An AC generator generates an alternating current when the current changes polarity during the generator's rotation however, a battery cannot "store" alternating current.

14. Procedural law is another kind of statutory law it is a body of rules that regulates the processing of an offender by the criminal justice system.

15. Roger Gould theorizes the natural progression of life that marks the path to adult maturity from ages 16 to 18 ages 18 to 22 ages 22 to 28 ages 29 to 34 ages 35 to 43 ages 43 to 50 ages 50 to 60.

16. Attorneys are responsible for the actions of their employees in both malpractice and disciplinary proceedings in the vast majority of the cases, the courts have not censured the attorneys for the particular act delegated to the legal assistant.

17. The drafting of legal documents in the absence of the attorney is not per se a violation of ethical standards the drafting process is not considered unsupervised as long as the attorney gives the work a stamp of approval before the client sees it.

18. Both the client and the nurse should evaluate the learning experience the client may tell the nurse what was helpful, interesting, and so on.

19. Most private security firms today depend on their own training programs to prevent actionable mistakes by their employees training in private security operations is also available from a number of schools and agencies.

20. All major battery manufacturers stamp codes on the battery case that give the date of manufacture and other information most battery manufacturers use a number to indicate the year of manufacture and a letter to indicate month of manufacture.

21. Some developmental pathologic conditions that affect the teeth include anodontia, a lack of development of the teeth supernumerary teeth, an excess number of teeth microdontia, teeth that are small in size and macrodontia, teeth that are large in size.

22. Exterior lighting is controlled by the headlight switch, which is connected directly to the battery on most vehicles therefore, if lights are left on, it can drain the battery.

23. Vehicles present a special law enforcement problem they are highly mobile, and when a driver is arrested, the need to search the vehicle may be immediate.

24. The term psychologic homeostasis refers to emotional or psychologic balance or a state of mental well-being it is maintained by a variety of mechanisms.

25. Shepard's Citations verify the current status of a known case, rule, or law for example, numbers in a Shepard Citation might look like: Part 1, page 701 Part 4, page 602 Part 17, page 411.

Colons

Colons are used to introduce a list, a statement, or to clarify or define a word. Most importantly, when you use a colon, a complete sentence <u>always</u> comes before the colon.

❧ *EXERCISE 6.2* ❧

Insert colons where appropriate (not every sentence will require a colon).

1. Paralegals are often asked to "brief" cases a short summary of a case with its primary points of law organized into a certain format.

2. The nursing process involves five major steps assess, diagnose, plan, implement, and evaluate.

3. Misdemeanors are relatively minor crimes consisting of offenses such as petty theft, simple assault, breaking and entering, possession of burglary tools, disorderly conduct, and disturbing the peace.

4. Airbags are known by many different names supplemental restraint system, supplemental inflatable restraints, supplemental air restraint.

5. There are several different ways to administer drugs orally, inhalation, topically, sublingually, injection, intravenous, and intramuscular.

6. The VPOINT commands contain four methods of entering a location including entering the three-dimensional, X,Y, Z coordinates, rotating the model through angles, rotating the model by use of a compass, and using preset locations.

7. When a circuit has more than one resistor of the same value in a series, there is a shortcut method to obtain the total resistance simply multiply the resistance value of the resistors having the same value by the number of equal-value resistors that are in a series.

8. In the 1990s, second generation digital access technologies were introduced TDMA, CDMA, and GSM.

9. Representative examples of horizontal exchanges include IMARK.com, Employease, MRO.com. BidCom, and YOUtilities.

10. The basic categories of voltmeters include the following electromagnetic, analog voltmeter, and digital voltmeter.

11. Command entry into AutoCAD can be accomplished in several ways using the command line through the keyboard, a pull down menu, a cursor context menu, a tool from the toolbar, a tablet menu, and a button menu.

12. The periodontium consists of those tissues that support tooth function including the gingival, alveolar bone, periodontal ligament, and cementum.

13. Older vehicles used a system to control evaporator pressure when used with a continually-operating compressor including a POA valve and an EPR valve.

14. Our legal system generally recognizes four broad categories of defenses alibis, justifications, excuses, and procedural defenses.

15. To implement the care plan successfully, nurses need special skills cognitive, interpersonal, and technical.

16. The court bailiff has many duties including being responsible for assisting the court, in maintaining order, custody of the prisoner while in court, and custody of the jurors.

17. The citation contains the location where the case may be found in the law library as well as other pertinent information the court, the district in which it was heard, and the year of decision.

18. Several positions are frequently required during physical assessment dorsal recumbent, horizontal recumbent, sitting, lithonomy, Sims', and prone.

19. One important measure of police success is strongly linked to citizen satisfaction response time.

20. All electrical circuits require three things to operate a voltage source, an electrical load, and a ground connection.

21. When cementing temporary crowns, the consistency and amount of cement placed in the temporary crown depends on one thing the type of crown to be seated.

22. Axonometric viewing makes use of orthographic techniques to view an object commonly known as parallel projection.

23. The unbalanced bridge is used to measure several types of physical quantities mechanical strain, temperature, or pressure.

24. Today's portals offer several functions search capability, access to specialized functions, personalization of content, and communities of interest.

25. The three endodontic instruments used in root canals are files, broaches, and reamers.

Dashes and Parentheses

The dash is an informal punctuation mark and is usually used to emphasize material. In addition, the dash introduces a list, a restatement, or clarification (In this sense, it is not unlike the colon whereby a complete sentence must precede a dash). While the dash emphasizes information, parentheses de-emphasize it. Parentheses are used to enclose material that the reader could skip over without missing the more important ideas.

⟨ EXERCISE 6.3 ⟩

Insert dashes or parentheses where appropriate.

1. The screw jack assembly sometimes called the gear nut is used to move the front or back of the seat cushion up and down.

2. Use the pen grasp for hand instruments explorers and spoon excavator.

3. The five goals of sentencing retribution, incapacitation, deterrence, rehabilitation, restoration represent a quasi-independent sentencing philosophy.

4. The wireless technology for cellular communications service transmits radio messages between a mobile device such as a mobile telephone, PDA, or wireless laptop and a cell site.

5. By observing the direction of the icon arrowhead, you can easily tell which way the X and Y axes are pointing see figure 4.6.

6. A nurse may require assistance because he or she is unable to implement the nursing activity safely on his or her own ambulating an unsteady obese client.

7. Points of law drawn from the case by the publisher called headnotes are important tools in helping the reader gain an insight into the contents of the case.

8. A radian rad is the angle formed when the distance along the circumference of a circle is equal to the radius of the circle.

9. The appellant may or may not be the one who "lost" in the lower court, since the "winning" party may have appealed only one particular aspect of the case such as the amount of damages.

10. The burden of care is frequently on women wives and daughters who are themselves aging.

11. The first step in proper viewing of a model is to identify the two crucial components of the center of interest the piece of the image at which the viewer is looking and the viewer's position in relation to the model.

12. A building containing a large proportion of steel or a room with line-of-sight obstacles or radio-wave absorbing materials such as cardboard or heavy fabric near an access point will likely cause disruption to wireless transmissions.

13. States operating under determinate sentencing guidelines often require that inmates serve a short period of time such as 90 days in reentry parole, a form of mandatory release.

14. The three kinds of film periapical, bitewing, and occlusal are manufactured in sizes 0-4.

15. A powerline capacitor also called a stiffening capacitor refers to a large capacitor of 0.25 farad or larger.

16. Biopsies to determine benign or malignant lesions are performed by surgically removing a small specimen of the abnormal tissue for further diagnosis.

17. Jailed women 12% of the country's jail population face a number of special problems.

18. In traditional forward auctioning sometimes called a Yankee auction shoppers make offers for a desired item.

19. You can save any view displayed in a viewport once saved it is easily restored.

20. Cyanosis a bluish tinge is most evident in the nail beds, lips, and buccal mucosa.

21. References to any appellate court decisions will usually include a series of numbers and abbreviations known collectively as a citation.

22. Wrong values in a circuit such as an incorrect resistor value can cause improper operation.

23. In the electrical utilities field, kilowatts kW and megawatts MW are common units.

24. The ethical guidelines governing the paralegal come from a variety of potential sources codes of ethics, statutes, and case law.

25. Boil water this is the most practical and inexpensive method to sterilize the home.

<u>Underlining and *Italics*</u>

Italics and underlining are the two accepted ways of designating published materials and other creative works. To determine if a work should be underlined, italicized, or put in quotation marks, consult a writing style manual (APA, MLA) or ask your instructor. Generally, however, book titles, comic strips, newspapers, magazines, anthologies, Web sites, music album/CD titles, television programs, movies, works of art (Mona Lisa, David), and names of ships (Queen Elizabeth II) are italicized or underlined.

❧ *EXERCISE 6.4* ❧

Underline in the appropriate places.

1. The Basics of Paralegal Studies by David Goodrich is the beginning text for paralegal studies.

2. For electronics, we use Electronic Fundamentals by Thomas Floyd.

3. Piaget's Origin of Intelligence in Children is a landmark text for understanding the different levels at which human beings progress.

4. AutoCAD in 3 Dimensions: Using AutoCAD 2004 was written to provide the information students need to compete in the job market.

5. The Home Depot has been voted America's Most Admired Retailer by Fortune magazine for many consecutive years.

6. According to Prisoners in 2000, the number of women incarcerated for drug crimes has risen 108% since 1990.

7. Information about dental assisting can be found in Richardson and Barton's The Dental Assistant.

8. Automotive Technology: Principles, Diagnosis, and Service by James Halderman and Chase Mitchell is organized around the eight automobile test areas.

9. The engine of the president's plane, Air Force I, is vastly different than that of an automobile engine.

10. The Running Man, a film with Dustin Hoffman, shows tooth extraction without lidocaine.

11. As written in "On-the-Job Stress in Policing" in the National Institute of Justice Journal (January 2000), stress is a natural component of police work.

12. With MIS Cases: Decision Making with Application Software by M. Lisa Miller, students will prepare to make management level decisions with the most complete and interactive management information systems casebook on the market.

13. AutoCAD resources can be found on www.autocad.com.

14. Peck's Psychological Aspects of Aging reveal psychological developments in the second half of life.

15. In 1975, the first personal computer was introduced by Altair, and Popular Science magazine featured it on the cover of the January 1975 issue.

16. Certified legal assistant information can be found by going to www.nala.org.

17. The electronics manual, Power On!, is a primary source of basic circuitry information.

18. Discussions of severe skin diseases can be found in Dermatology Nursing by R. Jackson.

19. The article, "Designing Your House," appears in AutoCAD Design for Today.

20. Losses from fraudulent and misleading business transactions conducted over the Internet are expected to reach $15 billion annually by 2005 according to a recent report in CIO Magazine.

21. "What Say Should Victims Have?" in Time magazine addresses victims' rights in the United States.

22. When I'm in the dentist's waiting room, I read the Dental Practice Management Encyclopedia.

23. A significant Internet resource for automotive technology is www.cars.net.

24. NYPD Blue is an accurate depiction of crime in New York.

25. Features titled Information Technology in Practice relate examples of successful IT use.

Quotation Marks

Quotation marks tell the reader that "someone is speaking or thinking." In addition, these marks are used with titles of chapters, essays, individual episodes of a TV series, newspaper articles, poems, songs, and short stories. Quotation marks can also signify "special" word usage.

⟨: *EXERCISE 6.5* ⟩

Add quotation marks where appropriate. Not all sentences deserve quotation marks.

1. The just deserts model of criminal sentencing insists that punishment should be the central theme of the justice process.

2. The dentist told the patient that wearing braces would be necessary to correct the gap between the front teeth.

3. My car, said the woman, is making noises like a washing machine.

4. The jury foreman told the judge that the defendant was guilty and should be put in jail for a hundred years.

5. My fail-safe computer system includes duplicate components; should one system malfunction, the other will take over to keep the computer running.

6. Mrs. Walters told the designer, Please include a pool room in my house. My husband she said, loves to play pool.

7. Feeling faint, the patient wobbled into the emergency room and whispered, Help me!

8. Paying Your Electric Bill which appeared in the <u>Washington Post</u>, helped me to understand the rising cost of electricity.

9. Procedural rules differ from one state to another, said the paralegal.

10. In his opening statement, the attorney told the jury that the defendant is non compo mentis.

11. The teacher asked if anyone had a question. Please explain bipolar voltage dividers to me, said the student.

12. The apothecary uses units of weight called the scruple, the dram, the ounce, and the pound.

13. In explaining parametric types, the teacher said, The parameters of a type 3ES parametric symbol allow it to be scaled uniformly in all three axes.

14. During the early days of information technology, the coming of the paperless office was proclaimed.

15. The Juvenile Justice Bulletin says that, Children who remain at large for a few weeks will resort to theft or prostitution as a method of self support.

16. NO! screamed the dental technician as the door opened. I'm developing X-Rays.

17. You're going to charge me WHAT? said the customer to the car repair technician.

18. When diagnosing any brake problem, claimed the boss, apply the parking brake and count the clicks.

19. Have you ever read the poem Ode to the Orthodontist?

20. She killed him in self-defense, said the attorney in his opening statement to the jury.

21. Backup procedures, also called backup copies, describe how and when to make extra copies.

22. The show, Home Improvement, is a long way from AutoCAD drafting.

23. I just love the song Doctor Cure All My Ills.

24. In explaining diodes, the electrician said that a diode is a semiconductive device made with a single pn junction.

25. The attorney told the paralegal, Some of your responsibilities will include interviewing clients, preparing court pleadings, and investigations.

❧ EXERCISE 6.6 ❧

Punctuate the paragraphs below, using as many forms of punctuation (comma, period, question mark, exclamation point, apostrophe, semicolon, colon, parentheses, quotation mark, dash, underline, and italic) as necessary.

A. Now that you've made the choice to enroll in college youve added new responsibilities to your life attending classes and studying to mention a few Your time is now even more limited Most likely you will find it difficult to do all that you used to without the help of those around you your employer family members friends teachers college peers and the college administrative staff Many adult college freshmen already have a strong network of family and friends Even if you live alone you can develop a strong support network through friends co workers and fellow students but to get help you must ask for it Make the choice to ask for help from all those who can give it to you

B. Stress and pressure two forces that most people deal with every day of their lives As adults youre already familiar with the feelings that stress can produce You're aware of what it means to cope with everyday pressures working paying bills meeting the needs of your family and friends making time for yourself and completing countless other tasks and obligations Now as an adult college student you may be wondering how you will be able to cope with adding the additional responsibilities of school studying attending classes tests to your already full plate You may be asking yourself how you will meet and deal with the many challenges that college will present While stress and pressure are natural parts of life you can learn to deal with these forces in productive ways You can make choices that will improve your physical health increase your energy and improve your attitude to help you through the collegiate process and to promote a better chance of success

C. Tests are not arbitrary lists of questions devised by instructors They are in fact well-organized structured and commonly formatted questions designed and developed to measure a students knowledge of a subject tests come in a variety of forms true false multiple choice short answer fill in and essay Each of these forms follows a predictable structure Recognizing and knowing these structures can aid in your ability to answer questions correctly and appropriately thus achieving a better grade In addition understanding the test format can reduce stress Youll know what to expect and how a particular type of test works Learning and comprehending the format and nature of different kinds of tests will make you more confident in your responses

D. Maximizing the classroom experience means being prepared for class participating actively in class and taking good class notes among other things But what if youre struggling with trying to take notes or what if you miss a class or two or what if personal issues distract you from paying attention in class Maximizing the classroom experience also means getting all that you can out of class If for whatever reason youre unable to get help if youre struggling with class ask teachers for direction tutors for assistance or fellow classmates for class notes A successful classroom experience relies on your ability to understand the material be prepared for class get the assignments and do the work if youre unable to get the help you need

E. Students who are not experienced in writing sometimes have misconceptions about the writing process They project certain ideas about writing papers that cloud their thinking and automatically establish obstacles to creativity and the writing process Perhaps because they were poor writers in high school some students believe that the college experience will be the same if previous teachers criticized papers and ideas then current college teachers will be just as critical Maybe some students tell themselves I cant write never could and never will Some college students tell themselves repeatedly they dont know how to write and cannot learn so why would they even want to try Maybe students believe that writing is no big deal Its easy enough to do it the night before the paper is due spend a couple of hours at the computer or maybe students believe that higher intelligence equals a better paper If Im smart then Ill get a better grade if Im not smart why would I want to put anything in writing in the first place Finally perhaps some students think that they will not ever have the need to write in their particular careers so why should they need to learn at all It is just these misconceptions about writing that prohibit you from writing It is just these false ideas about writing that inhibit your spontaneous abilities It is just these judgments about writing that halt your natural creativity and it is just these obstacles that prevent you from learning the skills you need to advance your career Now that youre in college you may want to reconsider your perceptions about written expression

Part IV
Grammar

Chapter 7
Agreement, Voice, and Qualifiers

Subject/Verb Agreement

Subject-verb agreement is based on one concept: The verb must agree in number (singular or plural) with the subject of the sentence.

General Verb Rules:

1. Generally (certainly not always), a singular verb in present tense is spelled with an 's' ending.

2. All past verb tenses, regardless whether the subject is singular or plural, are spelled the same.

General Subject Rules:

1. Generally, a singular subject requires a singular verb; a plural subject requires a plural verb.

2. Generally (certainly not always), a plural subject is spelled with an 's' ending.

3. Sentence subjects are always nouns (people, places, or things) or pronouns (replacements for nouns).

  Nouns as Subjects

  People

  - formal names: John, George Washington, Queen Latifah, the Beatles
  - informal titles: teacher, student, singer, president, fishermen

  Places

  - formal places: Des Moines, France, Jupiter
  - informal places: school, restaurant, beach, cities

Things

- animate objects: chair, computers, microbe

- inanimate objects: air, happiness, democracy

Pronouns as Subjects

- *Formal*: I, he, she, you (singular), we, you, they (plural)

- *Indefinite Singular*: each, either, neither, anybody, anyone, everybody, everyone, nobody, no one, somebody, someone, one, anything, everything, nothing, something, this, that, it

- *Indefinite Plural*: all, most

4. Joining two singular subjects with *and* requires a plural verb.

❧ *EXERCISE 7.1* ❧

Circle the subject and underline the correct verb in each sentence.

1. Immobility refer/refers to a reduction in the amount and control of movement a person has.

2. The most unique feature of the AIT format is/are the innovative emory-in-cassette drive interface system.

3. Criteria for a properly placed wedge require/requires that the wedge ensure stability of the matrix band.

4. The internal windings contain/contains approximately the same number of turns but are made from different gauge wire.

5. After the important distinction between primary and secondary authority is/are drawn, both state and federal material will be analyzed.

6. The Thevenin equivalent form of any two-terminal resistive circuit consist/consists of an equivalent voltage source and an equivalent resistance.

7. Every one of the areas in the blue cross-hatching represent/represents the effective plotting area.

8. Constitutive criminology refer/refers to the process by which human beings create an ideology of crime that sustain/sustains it as a concrete reality.

9. The Midtown Community Court in New York City show/shows how community courts work.

10. This list of radio buttons allow/allows you to tell AutoCAD what parts of your drawing you want to plot.

11. The sum of all the voltage drops around a single closed path in a circle is/are equal to the total source voltage in that closed path.

12. Either the attorney or the paralegal consult/consults with the plaintiff.

13. A thorough inspection of the spark plugs lead/leads to the root cause of an engine performance problem.

14. The main component of composite restorative materials is/are polymethyl methacrylate, hydrogen peroxide, calcium hydroxide, or inorganic filler.

15. The choice of cables affect/affects the network card.

16. A vesicle or blister cause/causes an erosion and illustrate/illustrates secondary lesions.

17. Each of the organisms cause/causes infection.

18. All the processing capabilities of the control unit and ALU reside/resides on a single computer chip.

19. Formation of tooth buds lead/leads to development of primary and succedaneous teeth.

20. Temperature or pressure controls prevent/prevents the freezing of the evaporator.

21. The group of nine justices is/are the highest court in the country.

22. The physical arrangement of components on a PC board bear/bears no resemblance to the actual electrical relationships.

23. The results of the rotation is/are dramatically affected by your choice of base point.

24. The number of new and innovative defenses being tried on juries and judges today is/are staggering.

25. In the Miranda decision, the Supreme Court require/requires that officers provide/provides warnings to potential criminals.

Active/Passive Voice

Using the *active voice* means that the subject of your sentence performs the action described by the verb as in, "The mechanic (subject) performed (verb) the annual maintenance on the car." In this sentence, the subject, *mechanic* performs the action described by the verb, *performed*. Rewritten in the *passive voice*, the sentence would read, "Annual maintenance (subject) on the car was performed (verb) by the mechanic." In the *passive sentence*, the subject of the verb is not acting, but is being acted upon. The subject, **maintenance** performs no action, but is being acted upon by the person who performs it. Notice also that a telling feature of the *passive voice* is the use of a helping verb (to be or to have). Using the *active voice* rather than the *passive voice* will make your writing clearer, more direct, and vital.

Rewrite the passive voice sentences below using the active voice.

1. Rules for contracts are contained in civil law.

    _____

    _____

2. Some explanation for creating polar rays is required.

    _____

    _____

3. The basic structure of a solenoid is shown in Figure 7-16.

    _____

    _____

4. Encyclopedias in appellate briefs or memoranda of law are not quoted directly by researchers.

    _____

    _____

5. Positive lubrication and long pump life are ensured when the oil pump is replaced after the engine is rebuilt.

    _____

    _____

6. The volume of gas administration to the patient is controlled by the flowmeter.

    _____

    _____

7. Instructions are not executed by the control unit.

    _____

    _____

8. The client's ongoing status should be described in the client record.

    _____

    _____

9. The most commonly used form of tape storage today are cartridges.

    _____

    _____

10. Emotional or psychological balance or a state of mental well-being is referred to as psychologic homeostasis.

_____

_____

11. All methods of examination—inspection, palpation, percussion, and auscultation—are included in an assessment of the lungs and thorax.

_____

_____

12. A monthly service fee is typically charged by ISPs.

_____

_____

13. Chemical mediators called hormones are produced by endocrine glands.

_____

_____

14. The voltage will drop in proportion to the resistance as stated by Kirchhoff.

_____

_____

15. A wide variety of cases are handled by the courts.

_____

_____

16. Higher capacitance values than mica or ceramic capacitors are offered by electrolytic capacitors.

_____

_____

17. An understanding of the relationships among model space, paper space, plot styles, page setups, and layouts is required in AutoCAD printing and plotting.

_____

_____

18. Based on their judgment and assessment, paroles are granted by parole boards.

_____

_____

19. The learning of convict values, attitudes, roles, and even language is referred to as prisonization.

_____

_____

20. Two commands for entering text in a drawing are provided by AutoCAD.

_____

_____

21. A general case of n resistors in parallel is shown in Figure 5-21.

_____

_____

22. Those who engage in certain kinds of behavior that unreasonably interfere with the rights of others or society as a whole are punished by our society.

_____

_____

23. The force produced by combustion chamber pressures and piston inertia to the channeling rod are transferred by the piston pin.

_____

_____

24. A rolling stroke and a vibratory stroke are incorporated by the modified Stillman technique.

_____

_____

25. As their CPU, specific microprocessor chips are contained by microcomputers.

_____

_____

Misplaced and Dangling Modifiers

Syntax in a sentence refers to the word order. To be understood by the reader, your sentence must make sense—it must flow in a logical and coherent way. Two problems that can create illogical or poor sentence syntax (and ambiguity) are _misplaced and dangling modifiers_. Look at these examples:

**Being so well known in the computer industry**, **I would appreciate your advice.**

**Because you are so well known in the computer industry**, **I would appreciate your advice.**

The italicized words are modifiers (words, phrases, or clauses) that give information about another word. In the first sentence above, there is no word to modify—the phrase dangles.

A misplaced modifier, on the other hand, means that the modifying word is in the wrong place as in:

I only paid $150.00 for this new computer. (**The word** *only* **should be placed as closely to the word it is modifying as possible.**)

I paid only $150.00 for this new computer. (logical placement of the modifying word)

⟨ *EXERCISE 7.3* ⟩

Rewrite the sentences below, altering the syntax by correcting and adjusting misplaced and dangling modifiers. (Note: not all sentences require rewriting.)

1. Grand juries served a far different purpose which was in the early days.

   _____

   _____

2. Just like the ones you have performed, the stretches require careful selection of multiple grips.

   _____

   _____

3. When a resistor is used in a circuit, its power rating should be greater than the maximum power that it will have to handle.

   _____

   _____

4. That index is organized alphabetically which may be several volumes in length.

   _____

   _____

5. Fuel injectors are usually controlled by varying the pulse width.

   _____

   _____

6. Wash your hands always with antimicrobial soap before and after you remove gloves.

   _____

   _____

7. Most PCs manufactured today have at least two USB ports built in, including laptop computers.

   _____

   _____

8. This technique is not used generally to percuss the thorax, but is useful in percussing an adult's sinuses.

_____

_____

9. If there are complaints of numbness, peculiar sensations, or paralysis, the practitioner should check sensation more carefully over flexor and extensor surfaces on the limbs of the patient.

_____

_____

10. Inserting or removing memory, chips, or boards changes the configuration of the computer, as well as storage or peripheral devices.

_____

_____

11. Always a nurse should assess a client's health status and obtain a medication history prior to giving any new medication.

_____

_____

12. Robots have moved from the realm of science fiction to the factory floor over the last few decades.

_____

_____

13. Clean tissue side of tray and disinfect always before seating in the patient's mouth.

_____

_____

14. If it does not feel or smell hot, it is possible that the problem is a faulty hot light sensor or gauge.

_____

_____

15. While addressing the traditional ways in which legal research is conducted, it is important to understand that there are now additional options available to the researcher as a result of widespread use of computers.

_____

_____

16. For the amplifier to operate properly, certain bias voltages must remain constant and, therefore, only remove any AC voltages.

_____

_____

17. The CHAMFER command sequence is identical almost to the FILLET command.

_____

_____

18. At the conclusion, the direct examiner may again question the witness.

_____

_____

19. These boxes all have a very similar format.

_____

_____

20. The ground points in a circuit are all electrically the same and are therefore common points.

_____

_____

21. When the decisions are rendered by a group of judges, the judges may not all agree with the conclusions or reasoning of the one writing for the majority.

_____

_____

22. A technician's hands should be always washed thoroughly after touching used engine oils, transmission fluids, and greases.

_____

_____

23. Being affected by either extrinsic or intrinsic stains, tooth bleaching is implemented primarily for aesthetics.

_____

_____

24. Systems have a practical limit to the number of all ports that can be added.

_____

_____

25. While exhaling, exert a gradual and gentle downward and forward pressure beneath the costal.

_____

_____

Chapter 8
Sentence Errors

Fragments

Our writing reflects our speech. If one speaks in fragments (partial sentences) or in run-on sentences (numerous combined ideas), then, one's writing will mimic this pattern. To correct this habit, remember that each sentence must have at least one independent statement with a noun and a verb. A sentence becomes unwieldy when several independent and dependent phrases or independent sentences are combined. To correct problem sentences, find the main noun and verb in each sentence and then decide if the remaining words are necessary or if added words will strengthen the sentence.

Examples:

- **Sentence fragment:** in the house, in the back of the room

  Sentence fragment written as a sentence: In the house, in the back of the room, lay the cat.

- **Run-on sentence:** In the house, in the back of the room, lay the cat that was snoring rather loudly mimicking a black bear in hibernation that is sleeping for the entire winter season.

  Run-on sentence written as two sentences In the house, in the back of the room, lay the snoring cat. The snoring mimicked a black bear in hibernation that is sleeping for the entire winter season.

⟨ EXERCISE 8.1 ⟩

In the first exercise, create full sentences from fragments. Before completing the sentence, analyze the fragment to determine which parts of speech to add. Once you have determined the missing part, add words that logically complete the sentence.

1. from the back of the operating room

   _____

   _____

2. moved from the dentist's office

   _____

   _____

3. visiting the dentist twice a year

_____

_____

4. stethoscope is used

_____

_____

5. screeching to a halt, the ambulance

_____

_____

6. your appointment, for now

_____

_____

7. use a syringe

_____

_____

8. clean, blue scrubs and masks

_____

_____

9. passing the forceps

_____

_____

10. pharmacy technicians, surgical technicians, and medical assistants

_____

_____

11. reviewing drawings and designs

_____

_____

12. animating the scene

_____

_____

13. designing a new room

_____

_____

14. plans for the garden

_____

_____

15. using 3D imagery

_____

_____

16. locating the tire jack

_____

_____

17. while driving through the neighborhood

_____

_____

18. than last year's model

_____

_____

19. cars waiting in line

_____

_____

20. drive shaft to be fixed

_____

_____

21. jails full of drug addicted criminals

_____

_____

22. hand-cuffs, bulletproof vest, gun, and mace

_____

_____

23. sentencing hearing to begin in the morning

_____

_____

24. patrolled the shopping mall parking lot

_____

_____

25. justice, swift and fair

_____

_____

26. watching the crime scene show on television

_____

_____

27. where the children play

_____

_____

28. felonies on the increase

_____

_____

29. career fair held last month

_____

_____

30. interviewing for the position

_____

_____

31. connecting the wiring for the fan

_____

_____

32. choosing the proper circuit board

_____

_____

33. avoiding water when blow drying your hair

_____

_____

34. ground the wires

_____

_____

35. knowing about reading voltmeters

_____

_____

36. defending the plaintiff

_____

_____

37. jury selection for tomorrow

_____

_____

38. real estate closings for the month

_____

_____

39. when the court opens

_____

_____

40. subpoenas to be served

_____

_____

41. weekly salary and benefits

_____

_____

42. career change

_____

_____

43. filled with pride

_____

_____

44. searching the classified advertisements

_____

_____

45. rushing to work yesterday

_____

_____

46. many people prefer

_____

_____

47. graduating from college this month

_____

_____

48. remember the lesson from last week

_____

_____

49. partially completed

_____

_____

50. eight-hour days for weeks

_____

_____

Run-on Sentences

❧ EXERCISE 8.2 ❧

In this exercise, re-write each run-on sentences as simple sentences. (The key to solving these is to find the two independent phrases that are represented by two different thoughts. Once you have found them, divide the phrases into two sentences. You may need to simply add a period to some or you may need to reword some).

1. The medical assistant left for work early in the morning and stopped for coffee at the coffee shop before driving to the office.

    _____

    _____

    _____

2. Working for others has always been difficult for her, so she has decided to be a contractor, which allows her to create her own schedule and to charge more money hourly.

    _____

    _____

    _____

3. Her cell phone rang many times before she was able to finish cleaning the patient's teeth so, she allowed it to ring even though it disturbed the dentist who was working next door.

_____

_____

_____

4. Often, the doctor asks for assistance when administering shots because he needs new glasses and so, cannot see the veins as well as before.

_____

_____

_____

5. The other night, Noah received a call from the night supervisor asking him to substitute for another technician, even though he had already worked the two shifts prior, he agreed.

_____

_____

_____

6. Before the ambulance could take the patient to the emergency room, the driver had to change the flat tire that was caused by a nail that the vehicle ran over.

_____

_____

_____

7. The patient called his dentist's office for an emergency appointment because he had an abscess that caused him tremendous pain and made him feel sick even though he realized its existence a week ago.

_____

_____

_____

8. After witnessing the fall, Georgia called the doctor to the hallway to help the patient who had passed out because she had not eaten before taking her medication earlier that morning.

_____

_____

_____

9. Where are the sutures and where are the forceps and do you know where the extra packages of gauze are?

_____

_____

_____

10. Now that I have completed my clinical rounds, I am eager to begin my search for a new job but I know that it will not be easy to find a job in this area of the country.

_____

_____

_____

11. Does anyone know when the updated drawing program will be available for us to test because we are working on a design that needs the new multi-creation feature so that we can show the client a variety of dimensions.

_____

_____

_____

12. While mapping the schematics for the power grid, the engineer discovered a design flaw created during the revision meeting with the clients that continued for hours though everyone was tired.

_____

_____

_____

13. Where are the plans for the outdoor deck, did you misplace them or are they, perhaps, in your car because we need them for this meeting.

_____

_____

_____

14. He reported that his truck broke down somewhere between two highway exits for the next town north, though he is uncertain as to the cause, he knows that the starter needs replacing.

_____

_____

_____

15. Oil changes are not difficult to complete unless you do not have the proper tools, then, it is impossible to do it properly; in fact, you could damage your engine.

_____

_____

_____

16. Last night, there was a violent windstorm in the mid-west whose destruction was so fierce that it levied damage upon town after town leaving thousands without power.

_____

_____

_____

17. Jayne called an electrician to install a ceiling fan and to install an additional electrical outlet in her house; he cannot come for another week which is problematic.

_____

_____

_____

18. Late to her advanced circuitry class, Sheila worried that she missed the review for the test that is to be given next Wednesday night and next Thursday night.

_____

_____

_____

19. Although there are better ways to connect the wires for the stereo, the technician insisted on using the factory speaker cables that were packaged with the system because he wanted to keep the cost of the job to less than one hundred dollars.

_____

_____

_____

20. The five steps in Thevenin's Theorem provide that an equivalent circuit can be used to replace the original circuit even when the circuits are slightly different from each other.

_____

_____

_____

21. We advised that the client purchase three laptops, two desktop computers, a server and five printers all of which will be networked together and will create an office that should allow staff members to work on projects separately in their own offices.

_____

_____

_____

22. Sometime between last night at 6:00 P.M. and this morning at 5:00, A.M., a virus attacked our operating system because when I arrived in the office at 6:00 A.M., I noticed that the screen, which should have displayed my screensaver, was blank.

_____

_____

_____

23. Excited about the release of the new beta software for the word processing program, the team anxiously completed the last data tests that are required before marketing it to the public.

_____

_____

_____

24. Please schedule an appointment with Mr. Mercado tomorrow since he has complained that his printer is not working properly and be sure to take an extra ink cartridge with you because I think that the problem is that the other one is empty.

_____

_____

_____

25. Has anyone seen the latest posting on the webpage because I heard that our company is featured as one of the hottest design firms in town and if that is true, we can create a link from our site to that one.

_____

_____

_____

26. I am frustrated because I have tried to upload my assignment for the past three hours and continue to receive the message that the server is busy or broken so the assignment partially loads and then seems to be stuck.

_____

_____

_____

27. Someone told me that I should schedule an appointment with a legal assistant to discuss my options for filing divorce because if I do not do this, I might not be able to keep most of my property.

_____

_____

_____

28. When we decided to purchase our home, we hired an attorney to review the closing documents because we had never bought a home before and wanted to be sure that we understood all of the language in the contract.

_____

_____

_____

29. The legal assistant spent most of the night conducting research for the trial scheduled for the following day because the attorney that he worked for discovered some new information that might be relevant.

_____

_____

_____

30. I heard that Ms. Lowry's torte class is very difficult and that she assigns a lot of homework and gives many tests because she believes that this helps students to learn the information.

_____

_____

_____

31. To find a job in my field, I need to use the Internet to research information about salary, location, and anything else that will help me to choose the best option: one that suits my values and my lifestyle preferences and will help me to earn more money than I am earning now.

_____

_____

_____

32. Before graduation, I am going to write cover letters and a resume so that I will be ready to search for a job and work in my field because I want to use my skills to help people who are working with the criminal justice system.

_____

_____

_____

33. My study skills have improved since enrolling in college classes because I have had to learn to write papers, organize my activities into a schedule, and conduct research and I know that these skills will help me to succeed in my career once I complete my degree requirements.

_____

_____

_____

34. Learning to write clearly, using proper grammar and punctuation can take time and practice and is necessary, I know, so that I will be able to write competently once I am working in my career.

_____

_____

_____

35. Many times I have considered withdrawing from my college classes because I felt overwhelmed by the work and the pressure of completing assignments by the deadlines and worrying about my grades but, somehow, I manage to complete everything and then feel better.

_____

_____

_____

Chapter 9
Sentence Connectors

Conjunctions

COORDINATING CONJUNCTIONS

Coordinating conjunctions (and, or, but, not, for, so yet) serve four specific functions: they

- join words together

  cellphones and computers, not cellphones but computers

- join phrases together

  Wade repairs electronic equipment, including cellphones and computers.

  Wade repairs some electronic equipment, including cellphones, but not computers.

- join independent sentences together

  Wade repairs electronic equipment and he is most proficient with cellphones.

  Wade repairs electronic equipment, but he is not proficient with cellphones.

- inform the reader that the words, phrases, or independent sentences you're joining have equal value

  accurate and precise (words)

  Steve's CAD drawings are accurate, but not precise. (phrases)

  Steve's CAD drawings are accurate, but he is not very precise. (independent sentences)

(It is important to note that by using a coordinating conjunction, you signal to the reader that the words, phrases, or sentences you're combining have equal value and meaning within the context of the whole sentence (accurate and precise). DO NOT USE a coordinating conjunction if the words, phrases, or independent sentences do not have equal value (cellphone and Ohm's law, computer and hypodermic needle).

⟨ EXERCISE 9.1 ⟩

Underline the coordinating conjunction(s) in the sentences below.

1. Written law is of two types: substantive and procedural.

2. The right button on your mouse can also be used in place of the Enter key sometimes, but in most cases, there will be an intervening step involving a shortcut menu with choices.

3. The curve showing how these two quantities (B and H) are related is called the B-II curve, or the hysteresis curve.

4. Problems in reducing an issue to written form may be an indication that the researcher has not yet clearly formulated the issue.

5. The belt is generally considered to be quieter, but it requires periodic replacement.

6. Fluoride toxicity is a potential danger if the correct dosage of fluoride is not administered, so be very careful.

7. Streaming also makes it possible for many users to retrieve the same file of audio, video, or other information simultaneously.

8. Characteristics of pit and fissure sealants include self-cured or light-cured polymerization and acid etching.

9. Neither engine oil nor break fluid should be applied to a Teflon oil seal.

10. Many, but not all, of the states have separate state reporters, and citations of cases in such states should contain references to both the state and regional reporters.

11. This particular instrument can be used to measure either direct current or alternating current quantities.

12. You can select individual entities on the screen by pointing to them one by one, yet in complex drawings this is often inefficient.

13. Criminal trials under our system of justice are built around the adversarial system and central to this system is the advocacy model.

14. Private attorneys either have their own legal practices or work for law firms in which they are partners or employees.

15. To define movement with a vector, all AutoCAD needs is a distance and a direction.

⟨ EXERCISE 9.2 ⟩

Add the appropriate coordinating conjunction to the sentences below.

1. The LCD requires little current, _____ it is difficult to see in low light _____ is slow to respond.

2. Any item, including custom trays _____ dental waxes, that has been used in the mouth carries the potential for cross contamination, _____ always disinfect or dispose of used materials.

3. You can also provide your own text, _____ that would defeat the purpose of setting up a coordinate system that automatically gives you the distances from the intersection of the two lines.

4. A person cannot be tried, sentenced, _____ punished while insane.

5. The appellees contend that there are literally hundreds of other pieces of property of the same size _____shape within the very same development _____ that the appellant therefore cannot establish the requisite uniqueness of the property, _____ this argument overlooks one very important factor.

6. Either the deglazing hone _____ the sizing hone is used for cylinder service.

7. Neither a desktop _____ laptop computer can ever replace the human brain.

8. Often, a section of the electronic component may be damaged, _____ will not fail until several days or weeks later.

9. On the basis of the judge's finding, the person is arrested _____ taken to a magistrate's hearing _____ notified of the pending charges, the right to counsel, _____ any potential adjustment of the amount set for bail, _____ there is no need for a preliminary hearing because the judge has already determined that probable cause exists.

10. The types of teeth are the incisors, canines, premolars, _____ molars.

11. Line operations are field _____ supervisory activities, _____ staff operations include support roles, like administration.

12. Remember, the procedure listed is a general list of how to enter _____ use the LINE command, _____ it is for reference and clarity only.

13. Air-core _____ ferrite-core transformers generally are used for high-frequency applications _____ consist of windings in an insulating shell that is hollow _____ constructed of the ferrite.

14. Neither cybercrime _____ information-technology crime was ever conceived of in the 1900s.

15. Supragingival calculus occurs above the gum line, _____ subgingival occurs below the gum line.

Part A-Join words together (in your field) in six different ways using the coordinating conjunctions: and, or, nor, but, so, yet. For example, heart and liver; pale yet breathing normally; blood or mucus; thin but healthy; inflamed so hot; hot nor cold; sick yet laughing.

Allied Health

_____ and _____

_____ or _____

_____ nor _____

_____ but _____

_____ so _____

_____ yet _____

AutoCAD

_____ and _____

_____ or _____

_____ nor _____

_____ but _____

_____ so _____

_____ yet _____

Automotive Technology

_____ and _____

_____ or _____

_____ nor _____

_____ but _____

_____ so _____

_____ yet _____

Criminal Justice

_____ and _____

_____ or _____

_____ nor _____

_____ but _____

_____ so _____

_____ yet _____

Electronics

_____ and _____

_____ or _____

_____ nor _____

_____ but _____

_____ so _____

_____ yet _____

Information Technology

_____ and _____

_____ or _____

_____ nor _____

_____ but _____

_____ so _____

_____ yet _____

Paralegal Studies

_____ and _____

_____ or _____

_____ nor _____

_____ but _____

_____ so _____

_____ yet _____

Part B-Next, join phrases together (in your field) in six different ways using the coordinating conjunctions: and, or, but, nor, so, yet. For example,

put on sterile gloves **and** clean the incision; apply a gauze wrap **or** an elasticized bandage; dress the wound **but** do not apply topical medicine; blood pressure **nor** vital signs; prepare patient **so** take vitals; calm, **yet** high blood pressure.

Allied Health

_____ and _____

_____ or _____

_____ but _____

_____ nor _____

_____ so _____

_____ yet _____

AutoCAD

_____ and _____

_____ or _____

_____ but _____

_____ nor _____

_____ so _____

_____ yet _____

Automotive Technology

_____ and _____

_____ or _____

_____ but _____

_____ nor _____

_____ so _____

_____ yet _____

Criminal Justice

_____ and _____

_____ or _____

_____ but _____

_____ nor _____

_____ so _____

_____ yet _____

Electronics

_____ and _____

_____ or _____

_____ but _____

_____ nor _____

_____ so _____

_____ yet _____

Information Technology

_____ and _____

_____ or _____

_____ but _____

_____ nor _____

_____ so _____

_____ yet _____

Paralegal Studies

_____ and _____

_____ or _____

_____ but _____

_____ nor _____

_____ so _____

_____ yet _____

Part C-Now, join whole sentences together (in your field) using the seven coordinating conjunctions: and, or, but, nor, for, so yet. For example,

> **Wash your hands, <u>and</u> observe appropriate infection control procedures. Take all precautions to be sterile, <u>or</u> the patient may develop an infection. The patient may consume clear liquids up to two hours before surgery, <u>but</u> he should not eat solid food; neither permit fluids <u>nor</u> food by mouth <u>nor</u> allow the patient to wear jewelry before surgery. Some patients may have elevated blood pressure before surgery <u>for</u> they are usually frightened before the procedure. Pain is usually greatest twelve to thirty-six hours after surgery, <u>so</u> nurses monitor patients carefully immediately after a procedure. Patients may feel fine immediately following surgery, <u>yet</u> they are required to remain in bed to ensure complete recovery.**

Allied Health

And_____

_____.

Or_____

_____.

But_____

_____.

Nor_____

_____.

For_____

_____.

So_____

_____.

Yet_____

_____.

AutoCAD

And_____

_____.

Or_____

_____.

But_____

_____.

Nor_____

_____.

For_____

_____.

So _____
_____ .

Yet _____
_____ .

Automotive Technology

And _____
_____ .

Or _____
_____ .

But _____
_____ .

Nor _____
_____ .

For _____
_____ .

So _____
_____ .

Yet _____
_____ .

Criminal Justice

And _____
_____ .

Or _____
_____ .

But _____
_____ .

Nor _____
_____ .

For _____
_____ .

So _____
_____ .

Yet _____
_____ .

Electronics

And_____

_____.

Or_____

_____.

But_____

_____.

Nor_____

_____.

For_____

_____.

So_____

_____.

Yet_____

_____.

Information Technology

And_____

_____.

Or_____

_____.

But_____

_____.

Nor_____

_____.

For_____

_____.

So_____

_____.

Yet_____

_____.

Paralegal Studies

And_____

_____.

Or_____

_____.

But_____

_____.

Nor_____

_____.

For_____

_____.

So_____

_____.

Yet_____

_____.

<u>Subordinating Conjunctions</u>

Subordinating conjunctions connect subordinate clauses (incomplete sentences) to main clauses (complete sentences) and show a relationship between them. The most commonly used subordinating conjunctions are: *where, whenever, because, unless, until, though, although, even though, while, before, after, as, as long as, whether, despite, provided, since, in, if,* and *as a result.* Generally, subordinate conjunctions,

- mean that the subordinate clause (incomplete sentence) has less importance than the main clause (complete sentence)

- used at the beginning of the sentence (incomplete sentence) place emphasis and more importance on the main clause (complete sentence)

  Despite the varieties of possible justifications, self defense is probably the best known.

- used in the middle of the sentence, does not place emphasis on either clause

  Self defense is probably the best known justification despite the varieties of possibilities.

- signify location (where, over), time (before, when, until, after, since, while), and condition (*as long as, although, unless, whether, provided, if*)

  When a perpetrator is arrested, he must be Mirandized.

- can combine two complete (related) sentences using the formula **subordinating conjunction + incomplete sentence (less important) + complete sentence (most important information)**

  The police officer made many arrests. He was not promoted. (two complete sentences)

  Even though the police officer made many arrests, he was not promoted. (subordinating conjunction + incomplete/less important sentence + complete/most important sentence)

  Even though he was not promoted, the police officer made many arrests (subordinating conjunction + incomplete/less important sentence + complete/most important sentence)

The police officer was not promoted even though he made many arrests. (subordinating conjunction in the middle)

⟨ *EXERCISE 9.4* ⟩

Underline the subordinating conjunction in the sentences below.

1. Before creating the plot area window, look at the Plot Scale panel on the right of the dialog box.

2. As you learned in this chapter, capacitors are used in certain types of amplifiers for coupling AC signals and blocking DC voltages.

3. If the defendant is found guilty, the defense attorney will be involved in arguments at sentencing.

4. The server may be required by state law to sign a document after the service of process has been affected.

5. Because of regulations, containers used to transport regulated waste must be identified with a red biohazard label.

6. Hypothermia may result when the body is exposed to severely cold temperatures.

7. During assembly of system boards, the leads of the microprocessor package are inserted into holes in the circuit board.

8. When the ignition switch is turned to the start position, the motion of the plunger into the solenoid causes the starter drive to move.

9. You can find any topic of interest on the computer since so many databases are now available.

10. Even though people who have narcolepsy sleep very well at night, they nod off several times a day.

11. Protective, visible light eyewear is required to protect the eyes from retinal damage because of the potential for physical harm.

12. Whenever the Constitution is subjected to interpretation by the Courts, the resulting court precedent may have the effect of "amending" the Constitution.

13. Changing fonts is a simple matter because there is much room for confusion in the use of the words style and font.

14. After the Miranda decision was handed down, some hailed it as ensuring the protection of individual rights under the Constitution.

15. Since each resistor has the same current through it, the voltage drops are proportional to the resistance values.

❧ EXERCISE 9.5 ❧

Add the appropriate subordinating conjunction in each sentence.

1. _____ the defendant is a first time felon, the judge may give him a lighter sentence.

2. _____ you save a drawing file, AutoCAD allows you to save different versions of the same drawing under different names.

3. One can be sued for breach of a contract _____ it is oral or written.

4. _____ you touch the patient's mouth, be certain you are wearing gloves.

5. Clearly state the priorities of care and care that is due _____ the shift begins.

6. Acceptance and processing of orders submitted by customers are _____ the most common activities of business.

7. _____ the air density is lower at high altitudes, the power that a normal engine can develop is greatly reduced.

8. Laptop computers can save battery power _____ the computer is in hibernation mode.

9. _____ efforts have been made to control the costs of health care, these costs continue to increase.

10. An action may or may not be regarded as a decision on the merits _____ it is dismissed.

11. _____ the patient carries dental insurance, payment should be collected at each visit.

12. _____ your array definition is complete, AutoCAD needs to know how far apart to place all these circles.

13. Vehicles present a special law enforcement problem _____ they are highly mobile.

14. _____ voltages must be measured at several points in a circuit, the ground lead can be clipped to ground at one point in the circuit and left there.

15. A sophisticated approach to biological theorizing about crime causation has arisen _____ the past few decades.

❧ *EXERCISE 9.6* ❧

Combine the sentences below using subordinating conjunctions in three (3) different ways:

    a. **subordinating conjunction + incomplete sentence and less important idea + complete sentence and most important idea**
       Oscar studied hard. He failed the test.
       <u>Even though</u> Oscar studied hard, he failed the test.

    b. **subordinating conjunction + incomplete sentence and less important idea + complete sentence and most important idea**
       Oscar failed the test. He studied hard.
       <u>Even though</u> Oscar failed the test, he studied hard.

    c. **complete sentence + subordinating conjunction + complete sentence**
       Oscar studied hard. He failed the test.
       Oscar failed the test <u>even though</u> he studied hard.

Allied Health: *Health care costs continue to increase. Efforts have been made to control health care costs.*

    a. _____

    _____

    b. _____

    _____

    c. _____

    _____

AutoCAD: *The spacebar is one of the oldest AutoCAD features. It is a major contributor to the goal of heads-up drawing.*

    a. _____

    _____

    b. _____

    _____

    c. _____

    _____

Automotive: *Seatbelts can be uncomfortable. Seatbelts can save your life.*

a. _____

_____

b. _____

_____

c. _____

_____

Criminal Justice: *He was sentenced to three years in prison. He was paroled after one year.*

a. _____

_____

b. _____

_____

c. _____

_____

Electronics: *Sean turned off the circuit breaker. He received a shock when he turned on the light switch.*

a. _____

_____

b. _____

_____

c. _____

_____

Information Technology: *Software companies continually update pieces of software. These companies need to let customers know.*

a. _____

_____

b. _____

_____

c. _____

_____

Paralegal: *Funeequa received a large settlement. She was delinquent on her bills.*

a. _____

_____

b. _____

_____

c. _____

_____

Parallelism

Parallelism means putting similar words, phrases, and ideas together in similar form. Parallelism repeats patterns of words (verbs, nouns, adjectives, and adverbs) and clauses to increase comprehension and improve writing style. Essentially, parallelism implies that when you begin a list format, you stay in the same form and structure. For example,

- *After completing this section, you should be able to describe a basic electrical circuit, relate a schematic, and describe various types of switches.* (parallel structure)

- *After completing this section, you should be able to describe a basic electrical circuit, understanding the schematic will be necessary too, and descriptions of various types of switches.* (not a parallel structure)

- *Safety precautions include reporting of unsafe conditions, wearing safety glasses, and keeping tools properly maintained.* (parallel structure)

- *Safety precautions include reporting of unsafe conditions, needing to wear safety glasses, and make sure you keep tools properly maintained.* (not a parallel structure)

- *Electrical current paths include touch potential, step potential, and touch/step potential.* (parallel structure)

- *Electrical current paths include touch potential, stepping potential, and something called touch/step potential.* (not parallel structure)

EXERCISE 7

Each group contains a word or phrase that is not parallel with the others. Change the incorrect word/phrase to the correct parallel form. Write the correct answer in the blank or OK if the words/phrases are parallel.

1. researching law, drafting documents, to interview witnesses, organizing evidence

    _____

2. press, indicate, answering, move _____

3. feelings about self, reactions from others, one's perceptions of these reactions, attitudes, values, many of life's experiences _____

4. troubleshoot series-parallel circuits, determine the effects in a short circuit, locating opens and shorts_____

5. incisors used for biting, canines used for tearing, use premolars and molars for crushing and to grind _____

6. reliable, economical, compact, convenience _____

7. victims experience uncertainties, traumas, and fear _____

8. intake or exhaust valve, piston rings, cylinder head gasket _____

9. enforcing the law, apprehending offenders, prevent crime, preserving the peace, provide services _____

10. to manage detail, to give a common meaning, to document features, locate errors

    _____

11. proteins, carbohydrates, fats, minerals, vitamins, water _____

12. define resistance and discuss its characteristics, name and define the unit of resistance, describing the basic types of resistance, determine resistance value

    _____

13. quiet the mind, focusing on the present, releasing anxieties about the future

    _____

14. beginning a new drawing, draw a vertical line, typing the line_____

    _____

15. deliberation, premeditation, solicitation _____

    _____

Rewrite the following sentences putting them in parallel form.

1. Prior to trial, the paralegal may be called upon to locate and contact all witnesses, organize court pleadings, and he may be requested to accompany the attorney to trial.

   _____

   _____

   _____

   _____ .

2. The procedure for entering multiline text using MTEXT includes typing t, specify the first corner, typing the text, and click OK.

   _____

   _____

   _____

   _____ .

3. Explain to the patient what you are going to do, why it is necessary for him, and how he or she can cooperate with you.

   _____

   _____

   _____

   _____ .

4. In a case of a short in the circuit, a faulty wire clipping, solder splash, or some bad touching leads is found to be the problem.

   _____

   _____

   _____

   _____ .

5. The bone that supports the teeth is called the alveolar bone or it's called the cancellous or the medullary bone.

_____

_____

_____

_____ .

6. The participants may be in the same room, or they could be linked up by a local area network, or geographically dispersed and interconnected over a wide area network.

_____

_____

_____

_____ .

7. The type of intermediate sentencing the judge imposes is based on whether the offender committed the crime out of a need for money, for the excitement it afforded, because he wanted revenge, or for "the thrill of it."

_____

_____

_____

_____ .

8. To perform an accurate compression test, remove all spark plugs, then make sure you block open the throttle and the choke, and next, thread a compression gauge into one spark plug and crank the engine.

_____

_____

_____

_____ .

9. Laws serve a variety of purposes including preventing the victimization of innocents, sustain existing power relationships, upholding established patterns of social privilege, and maintain values.

_____

_____

_____

_____ .

10. Information technology professionals are responsible for acquiring development, maintenance, or operations of the hardware and software associated with computers and communications networks.

_____

_____

_____

_____ .

11. Sodium fluoride 2% offers many advantages: it does not stain teeth; it remains a stable solution when stored in a polyethylene bottle; there is a less objectionable taste when you use it; gingival irritation does not occur.

_____

_____

_____

_____ .

12. Capacitor values are indicated on the body of the capacitor by numerical labels or phanumerical labels or sometimes they use color codes.

_____

_____

_____

_____ .

13. Normally, older clients have unaltered perception of light touch and superficial pain, as well as a decreased perception of deep pain, and they have a decreased perception of temperature stimuli.

_____

_____

_____

_____ .

14. The SPLINEDIT command gives you additional options, including the option to change the tolerance, adding fit points for greater definition, or deletion of unnecessary points.

_____

_____

_____

_____ .

15. It is unethical for paralegals to enter into partnerships, or associations, or even corporations with attorneys in a business involving the practice of law.

_____

_____

_____

_____ .

16. Dimensions can be edited in many of the same ways other objects are edited; they can be moved, copied, stretched, or sometimes they can be rotated, include trimming, and they can be extended too.

_____

_____

_____

_____ .

17. The infection control nurse records and analyzes statistics, may be involved in employee education and implementation of the mandated OSHA plan.

_____

_____

_____

_____ .

18. Troubleshooting involves applying logical thinking, making sure you have a thorough knowledge of circuits, and to form a logical plan of attack.

_____

_____

_____

_____ .

19. The substance within the bone, known as bone marrow, produces red blood cells, also platelets, and white blood cells as well.

_____

_____

_____

_____ .

20. The basic purposes of policing in democratic societies are enforcing and supporting the laws of society, to investigate crimes and to apprehend offenders, preventing crime, help to ensure domestic peace and tranquility, and making sure to provide the community with needed enforcement-related services.

_____

_____

_____

_____ .

Chapter 10
Pronoun Usage

Pronoun Agreement

Use a pronoun to refer to a noun (antecedent) in a sentence. Sometimes, the antecedent is a proper noun, such as in "Martha went to the store because she ran out of milk." **She** refers to **Martha** in the sentence meaning that Martha is the antecedent. There are also instances when the antecedent may be an indefinite noun. For example, "**Both** decided to offer Rob the job because they believed that he was the best candidate for the job." In this sentence, the word **they** refers to **both**. Remember to follow these rules when working with pronouns:

- The pronoun must agree with its antecedent; plural antecedents must correspond to a plural form of the pronoun.

- Be certain that the pronoun refers to the proper antecedent. Unclear reference will cloud the meaning of your sentence.

- Be certain that the pronoun's point of view matches other pronouns: first person reference should be used throughout the sentence.

❧ EXERCISE 10.1 ❧

Underline the antecedent in each sentence below and write an A above the antecedent. (In some cases, there may be more than one). Then, underline the pronoun and write a P above the corresponding pronoun. When you find two antecedents, mark one as A1 and the other as A2; do the same with the pronouns. This will assist you in identifying the connection between the two types of words. For example,

I need your lug wrench because it fits the car's engine better than mine does.

A1   A2   P2   P1

I need your lug <u>wrench</u> because <u>it</u> fits the car's engine better than <u>mine</u> does.

1. George spent last night completing his writing assignment for his case law class.

2. To date, Charlie has not encountered a problem like this; he is uncertain of how to fix the

   programming error.

228

3. Interviewing is not an easy process because it challenges people to use quick thinking.

4. Mario, Shawntee, and Jack are going to the conference to demonstrate their robotic arm model.

5. The driver watches the road signs carefully so that he will not miss the turn.

6. Whenever Steve discussed the movie project, he argued about whether the animation should be in 2D or 3D.

7. The schedule indicates that May is enrolled in the four classes that she needs for graduation.

8. Remember to wear your scrubs for class on Monday, because you will be going to the hospital to watch an operation.

9. Torte law is not a difficult subject to study, though it can be if you do not complete your readings before class.

10. It is somebody else's job to complete the paperwork though he/she may not be aware of that.

11. Worried about the trojan virus on his computer, Vinnie called the company's computer technician for assistance.

12. Juana learned that she is to be promoted next week because of her excellent work as a probation officer.

13. The electrician, puzzled because he could not find the short in the circuit, decided to test all of the circuits

14. Patricia started the car this morning to find that it blows smoke from the tailpipe.

15. Today, James is being released from the detention center; he wants to thank his counselor, Pedro, for helping him.

16. Frank created the designs for the house; he is proud of them.

17. During the violent windstorm, some electrical poles fell as they had been loosened by past storms.

18. Please, ask someone to review your resume before sending it to companies.

19. Hard work and perseverance helped Jim to excel in his studies; he will continue to work like this on his job.

20. Keisha cannot decide whether she should work in a hospital or in a doctor's office.

⟨ EXERCISE 10.2 ⟩

In the sentences below, circle the pronoun that matches the antecedent. Decide if the antecedent is singular or plural and then choose the equivalent pronoun.

1. Working in the garage allows Manuel to practice the skills that (they, he) learned in school.

2. Both felt that the proposed revisions enhanced the project, for this reason, (they, he/she) wanted to meet with the client to gain his approval.

3. Mary struggled to complete (she, her) designs for the new kitchen.

4. Anyone can change the oil in a car as long as (they, he/she) understands all of the steps involved.

5. When did the schemata change? Someone must have discovered a problem with the plans and decided that (he/she, they) would make the adjustments.

6. Michael, Liza, and Debbie decided that (they, he/she) would study their anatomy together in the media center.

7. (We, Us) five will work in the emergency wing this evening to complete our clinical rotations.

8. The four of (we, us) considered applying for positions as legal assistants in the same law firm.

9. Sharona collected the surgical tools and took (them, it) to the operating room to be laid on the table.

10. Research can be tedious to collect because (it, they) requires meticulous attention to detail.

11. The truck buckled from the added weight of the bricks, (it, they) are heavier than anticipated.

12. Janet met with the client to discuss the estimate for wiring the house; (it, she/he) will be a difficult job.

13. Has everyone decided what (he/she, they) want(s) to study in college?

14. We decided that either of you can work with the next patient as long as (you, he/she) check(s) with the dentist before dismissing the patient.

15. Nobody would confess that (they, he/she) forgot to write the notes on the patient's chart.

⟪ EXERCISE 10.3 ⟫

In this exercise, fill in the blank with an appropriate pronoun. (Be sure your choice matches the antecedent, if there is one). Also, make sure the pronouns agree in number (singular or plural).

1. Our last surgical procedures class ended last Tuesday. _____ are excited about the

prospect of working in a hospital in the operating room. There are so many operations

that _____ did not have the opportunity to assist with during _____ internships.

Personally, I am eager to use _____ new skills to assist surgeons.

2. The patient needs to lie in the prone position on the table. _____ will then be asked to lie still as the nurse takes _____ blood pressure and vital signs. _____ will only take a few minutes to complete the procedure. We will then meet in the lab to view _____ x-rays that were taken last week; _____ should help _____ to make a diagnosis.

3. We learned in _____ career skills class that in order for _____ to be offered the jobs that _____ want, _____ have to write clear resumes. Writing _____ was difficult for each of us since we had not written resumes before. Resumes, in order to be effective, must contain _____ education and work experience. I was pleased with _____ when I finished.

4. While driving home from the market, one of my tires drove over a nail. Now, _____ was flat and _____ had to change _____ before _____ could return home with the groceries. Not remembering how to change a flat tire, I called my mechanic for assistance. _____ told _____ to use my car jack to raise the car. Next, _____ used a wrench to loosen the lug nuts, one of _____ took a long time to remove. Tired from the effort, I rested against the car, _____ was still warm. It was then that I remembered that the food was still in the car. _____ was worried that the frozen goods would melt. So, I opened the ice cream to check. _____ tasted so good, that _____ finished the whole container before finishing _____ work with the tire.

5. The architect called to see if the plans were completed. _____ needs _____ for the presentation tomorrow. If the dimensions are not correct, then revisions will be necessary. _____ is not enough time for major revisions, however. We created the plans using the specifications given to _____.

6. The receptionist advised me that a woman was waiting to see _____. When _____ was

ready to meet with _____, the receptionist brought _____ to _____ office. I motioned for

_____ to sit in the chair across from _____ and asked _____ for information about the

case. _____ disclosed that _____ was cheating on _____ husband and wanted to leave

_____. _____ explained the divorce filing process to _____. She decided that _____ would

consider our discussion before finalizing her decision to start the divorce proceedings.

7. "Quiet! _____ have the right to remain silent, anything that _____ say can and will be

used against you in a court of law." As the officer finished mirandizing the criminal,

_____ noticed three men approaching. The officer waited warily as the men came closer,

wondering if _____ would attack. Not wanting to risk an altercation, the officer worked

quickly to secure the criminal in the cruiser. After starting the car, the group passed

without incident. Breathing a sigh of relief, the officer wondered if _____ was time to

schedule a vacation!

8. Excitedly, the group of students discussed graduation plans. _____ discussed _____ future

career goals and present job searches. One woman announced that _____ would start a

new job working in an animation studio beginning next Monday. Another woman

commented that _____ was still attending interviews to work as a legal assistant. Two

men, both graduating with honors, stated that _____ were going to start a consulting

business together. All concluded that _____ could not wait to use _____ experience and

education in new careers.

9. Someone called to complain that _____ does not have power in _____ house. Before we send a team of linemen to the area, can _____ check to see if there are other reported outages? Please check the grid for that area and report back to _____.

10. Please check the gaskets to see if _____ still fit tightly. If _____ is not coming from there, then try to follow the leak through the engine. Look for the areas that have the most oil, _____ will find the source of the leak.

⟨ EXERCISE 10.4 ⟩

This, that, these, those, and it are all pronouns which refer to antecedents as other pronouns do. When used without a specific referent, the reader is uncertain as to the meaning of the sentence because the pronoun does not refer to anything specific (the antecedent). For example, "It was a harrowing experience!" is less specific than "Tipping over in our boat was a harrowing experience!" Rewrite the sentences below following the above example. Change "this, that, these, those, and it" to refer to specific items, people, and events. In some instances, more than one indefinite pronoun needs to be replaced.

1. It was difficult in class yesterday.

   _____
   _____

2. Please, pass that to me. I need it to fix this.

   _____
   _____

3. Then, I noticed it. Please let me know what you intend to do about this.

   _____
   _____

4. Where is it? I believe that I left it at your house yesterday.

   _____
   _____

5. In the operating room, you had better have everything set for the surgeon. If you do not, it will delay the operation.

   _____
   _____

6. This is wonderful! Continue working this hard.

_____

_____

7. These are the most difficult for us to complete on time; ask for an extension on the deadline.

_____

_____

8. Oh no, those will not fit.

_____

_____

9. Could you please pass it to me?

_____

_____

10. That is exactly what we are seeking.

_____

_____

11. To date, the law briefs were written well. This, however, is not acceptable.

_____

_____

12. Greg thought that this would be the answer to our problem.

_____

_____

13. The students spent much time searching for it.

_____

_____

14. The 3D drawings showed imagination; these do not.

_____

_____

15. You are correct. That will conclude the opening argument.

_____

_____

Sometimes, we want to refer to more than one person using pronouns. In the next exercise, underline the appropriate pronoun.

1. He and (I/me) will attend the medical equipment convention in Reno next week.

2. She received her report card in the mail and saw that she earned straight A's; she is very pleased with (her/herself).

3. (We/Us) two team members are scheduled to work that shift.

4. The designs are exactly as (we/us) expected them to be; he and (me/I) worked hours trying to choose the proper gradient for the roof.

5. Between you and (me/I), many others have not handed in a paper yet.

6. He kept the secret to (himself, hisself).

7. My carburetor is not working properly, so I took the car to Michael and Jose's shop so that (them, they) can fix it.

8. (Her/She) and I are going to diagnose the patient together so that I can learn.

9. Our instructor divided the class into teams of (they/them) and (us/we).

10. While wiring the ceiling fan, (she/her) and (I, me) discovered that the hot wire was worn.

11. Knowing that the attorney values education, I decided to enroll in college to better (myself, me).

12. Please pass those screwdrivers to me, I believe that (they, them) are mine.

13. Larry and I arrived early for the premiere of our new animated short film, (us/we) are proud of (ourselves, us).

14. Thank you, but I believe that the credit is (yours, yourself).

15. Writing reports late at night is not a good idea because (us/we) spend too much time talking about the day. So, the reports are not (our, us) best work.

16. Oh, that V8 engine belongs to (he/him) and (I/me).

17. The doctor told (she/her) to take good care of (herself, her).

18. (Her/She) and (I/me) decided to apply for the same job. Then (we/us) decided to reward (uselves, ourselves) for taking such a step.

19. Check on that program to see if it fixed (themselves, itself).

20. It was decided that (we, us) would throw a large graduation party so that all can celebrate together.

Chapter 11
Word Usage

Troublesome Words and Homonyms

Word usage, or more specifically, improper word usage, can present difficult problems, especially in the case of homonyms (words that sound alike but are spelled differently). While the computer spell checker can tell you that a word is misspelled, it cannot tell you if you've used the right word in the right context. For example,

> *Ohm's Law is the <u>principle</u> law of electric circuitry.* (incorrect)

> *The <u>principal</u> law of electric circuitry is Ohm's Law.* (correct)

Improper word usage also presents problems in choosing an incorrect word in context. For example,

> *The defense attorney is the person <u>that</u> defends the accused.* (incorrect)

> *The defense attorney is the person <u>who</u> defends the accused.* (correct)

❧ *EXERCISE 11.1* ❧

In the sentences below, underline the appropriate word.

1. Currently, (they're, their, there) is no licensing of paralegals in any state.

2. Notice (to, too, two), that when specifying the rotation angle, the original orientation of the selected object is taken to be 0 degrees.

3. When the camshaft is installed, you (than, then) coat the lobes with a special lubricant.

4. If (your, you're) a crime victim, (you're, your) rights have been violated.

5. Strips of boxing wax are used to form a rim around an impression (that, which) contains the poured gypsum material.

6. The department's goal is (two, to, too) put all of (it's, its) aircraft manuals on CD-ROM.

7. By using larger cells, (that, which) have a larger quantity of material, the ability to supply current can be increased but the voltage is not (affected, effected).

8. For risk diagnosis, (now, no, know) subjective and objective signs are present.

9. The difference in energy levels is (quiet, quite, quit) smaller (then, than) the difference in energy between shells.

10. People collect data and information because they expect it to be useful later (whether, weather) to identify drivers, to diagnose and treat medical problems, or to train employees.

11. A developmental pathologic condition (that, which) can (effect, affect) the teeth is anodontia.

12. A prisoner's sentence can be reduced (thorough, threw, through, thru) parole.

13. To (insure, ensure) proper electrical connection (to, too, two) the inflator module in the steering wheel, a coil assembly is used in the steering column.

14. Drawing an isometric (plain, plane) in AutoCAD is an advanced skill.

15. (Its, It's) necessary to determine (weather, whether) the location is appropriate before asking for a change of venue.

16. If (you're, your) combinations of viewpoints are associated with one another, you can group them into a viewpoint configuration for easy redisplay.

17. If (their, there, they're) lightly scored, the clearances in the pump should be measured.

18. The law is like a living thing (that, which) (affects, effects) change over time.

19. Many companies have (they're, their, there) own local or regional training (sights, cites, sites) designed to train beginning service technicians and to provide update training (four, for, fore) existing technicians.

20. You will be able to rotate the (plain, plane) of your model so that you can see (you're, your) model as you change (your, you're) view of it.

21. You can (excess, access) the command by typing it on the command line.

22. The last tool generates camera views (which, that) is explained (farther, further) in later chapters.

23. The employer for (whom, who) the paralegal works must (except, accept) ultimate responsibility and accountability for the work of the legal assistant in his or her office.

24. Most large dealerships employ service technicians (that, which, who) are highly skilled.

25. Expert witnesses must demonstrate their expertise (thru, thorough, threw, through) education, work experience, publications, and awards.

26. A caustic substance (that, which) comes in contact with the eyes is (quit, quiet, quite) serious; if it happens, flush (you're, your) eyes with water immediately, (then, than) seek medical attention as quickly as possible.

15. After working all night, Ellen went home to crash before having to report back to the police station.

_____

_____

16. Rather than losing her temper all the time, she really needs to chill.

_____

_____

17. I heard that the other technician is a real drama queen; too bad you have to work with her.

_____

_____

18. The hospital where we completed our internship is a real dive.

_____

_____

19. Have you seen his new ride? I hear that it used to be a mess, but now, it is so sweet!

_____

_____

20. Yesterday's meeting was so whack; the client said that our work was tight.

_____

_____

❧ *EXERCISE 11.3* ❧

Colloquialisms are phrases used in informal speech. These phrases are not appropriate for formal writing. Rewrite the following sentences changing the informal language to formal.

1. I think that she's missing a few marbles.

_____

2. He reported that he is as happy as a clam at high tide.

_____

3. She's a tall drink of water.

_____

4. If you don't complete this project, you are digging your own grave.

_____

5. Martha reminded us that we shouldn't look a gift horse in the mouth.

_____

6. Don't judge them until you've walked a mile in their moccasins.

   _____

7. You can lead a horse to water but you can't make it drink.

   _____

8. A body can't get a minute's peace around here.

   _____

9. What does that have to do with the price of tea in China?

   _____

10. His tongue flaps like a dog's tail.

    _____

Answer Key

Part I: The Writing Process
Chapter 1: Writing Methodologies

EXERCISES 1.1-1.10: Because of the nature of the individual writing process, answers will vary.

EXERCISE 1.11:

Allied Health: 5, 7, 6, 9, 2, 1, 3

Kozier, Barbara, et al. *Fundamentals of Nursing.* 7th ed. Upper Saddle River, New Jersey: Prentice Hall, 2004. 364.

AutoCAD: 3, 6, 4, 7, 1, 8, 5, 2

Dix, Mark, and Paul Riley. *Discovering AutoCAD 2004.* Upper Saddle River, New Jersey: Prentice Hall, 2004. 246.

Automotive Technology: 4, 2, 6, 5, 1

Halderman, Mitchell. *Automotive Technology.* Upper Saddle River, New Jersey: Prentice Hall, 2004. 362.

Criminal Justice: 5, 8, 9, 3, 6, 1, 7

Schmalleger, Frank. *Criminal Justice Today.* Upper Saddle River, New Jersey: Prentice Hall, 2004. 106.

Electronics: 5, 1, 6, 2, 8, 4, 9, 10, 7

Floyd, Thomas L. *Electronics Fundamentals.* 6th ed. Upper Saddle River, New Jersey: Prentice Hall, 2004. 300.

Information Technology: 5, 8, 2, 6, 4, 1

Senn, James A. *Information Technology: Principles, Practices, Opportunities.* 3rd ed. Upper Saddle River, New Jersey: Prentice Hall, 2004. 60.

Paralegal Studies: 9, 4, 7, 1, 8, 5, 2

Goodrich, David Lee. *The Basics of Paralegal Studies.* 4th ed. Upper Saddle River, New Jersey: Prentice Hall, 2004. 106.

EXERCISE 1.12:

A. In an *ideal* world, people will do *what* they *are supposed* to, but people are people. *D*espite good *intentions,* things don't always work out the way *we'd* like them to. Even though your *friends* and family may be aware of *your* need to study for a test or write a paper, they may still ask you to *accompany* them *somewhere. (eliminate dash)* Sometimes it *(eliminate extra word)* is *necessary* to say "no" to people!!!!!!!!!!*(eliminate exclamation points and use a period)* Sometimes saying NO *no*!!$)**^#??//! *(eliminate all forms of punctuation) is* the only way you can *complete* college *assignments. S*aying "*no*" need not be a bad or negative word _,_ but *merely* a way to *assert your* need *to* do the work you need to do to complete your long range goal. *eliminate period w*hich you need to do if you want to graduate. If you need to say "no _,_" say it in a *positive* and *reassuring* way _._ *R*emind family and *friends* that school, takes *precedence* over what they might want from you. For their benefit. *(replace period with comma)* you need to study, *(eliminate 'don't you')* so that you can *pass* the test so that you can *pass* the class so *that* you can get the degree so that you can get the job you want so that you can improve the *quality* of your life and theirs.

B. *Critical* thinking is a skill *based* in logic and reason. *(replace period with comma) w*hich when applied to any and all situations, *conditions*, and *issues*, can *improve* the *quality* of *your* personal and *professional* live *life*? *(replace question mark with period)* Critical thinking can aid in resolution- *(replace dash with comma)* conflicts, *problem* solving _,_ communicating more *(eliminate "more")* effectively managing your *(eliminate "your") time*, taking tests, and even improve *your relationships. (eliminate "which we could all use"* Unfortunately _,_ because, *(eliminate comma)* many of us lack the skills of good critical thinking, we're relegated to responding to most *situations*, and people, in purely *emotional* ways. *replace question mark with period)* I*f however you learn *to use* the skills of critical thinking _,_ you can become more sucessful *successful* students _,_ *friends, and* employees.

Part II: Writing Styles
Chapter 2-Narration

Narrative Writing

EXERCISE 2.1: To answer the prompts in this exercise, use first person or active third person voice. Remember to use action verbs rather than passive ones; these will create movement in the story. Individual answers will vary.

EXERCISE 2.2:

Allied Health

2, 5, 1, 3, 6, 4

AutoCAD

3, 5, 1, 2, 6, 4

Automotive Technology

5, 1, 3, 4, 6, 2

Criminal Justice

3, 1, 4, 6, 2, 5

Electronics

2, 4, 1, 6, 5, 3

Information Technology

4, 3, 1, 6, 2, 5

Paralegal Studies

6, 2, 1, 5, 3, 4

EXERCISE 2.3: *These are suggested topic sentences that would introduce each of the corresponding paragraphs. Of course, any other response that provides an introduction to the proceeding information is correct.*

Allied Health

The ambulance parked behind the building to rush the patient to the operating room for an emergency bypass.

AutoCAD

Finally, I was able to reach Mr. Henderson to ask about a possible internship position with the company.

Automotive Technology

"This car does not look as if it has too many good miles in it."

Criminal Justice

Horrified, I watched the truck rush towards the intersection.

Electronics

I don't think that I sat down even once today; there is so much work for us to complete.

Information Technology

Excitedly, I installed the Internet browser and fire wall software.

Paralegal Studies

Working day and night researching this case, I decided to complete the last bit of work in the law library.

EXERCISE 2.4: For this exercise, be sure that the last sentence concludes the paragraph's information. The supplied endings are suggested conclusions; any sentence that logically completes the paragraph using narration is correct.

Allied Health

So, to make this decision, I need to decide whether a higher salary or scheduling flexibility is more important to me.

AutoCAD

She commented that while the background was striking, I mixed too many elements together.

Automotive Technology

Now, I need to decide if I want to change the exterior color in order to save $150.

Criminal Justice

It was then that I noticed that the garage was empty and that the car was missing!

Electronics

Despite my nervousness, I will attempt to complete my homework which involves working with a circuit board.

Information Technology

With the directions, I will still be able to arrive in time for my interview.

Paralegal Studies

Immediately, I found my attorney to report that I cannot work on this case with him because of my prior experience with the client.

EXERCISE 2.5: To answer this exercise effectively, write the topic and concluding sentences to introduce and complete the information given. The following answers represent one set of options. The first sentence in each pair represents the topic sentence with the second representing the conclusion.

Allied Health

1. Deep in discussion as we walked on the street, we watched a woman collapse on the sidewalk.

2. Thankfully, they revived her before transporting her to the hospital.

AutoCAD

1. Roaming the store, I searched for a small appliance to use with our design project.

2. This will be the first class project that challenges us to plan, draw, and design blueprints for something other than buildings.

Automotive Technology

1. Ms. Lopez returned the car this afternoon complaining that it still stalls and lurches without warning.

2. I think that we are going to have to replace the charging system because the battery is damaged.

Criminal Justice

1. Since he may return tonight, even though we have officers looking for him, it is unsafe for you to stay here tonight.

2. But, I do not feel comfortable leaving you here; you are in danger!

Electronics

1. Unsure about my job options once I graduate from college, I scheduled an appointment to meet with a career counselor to explore possibilities.

2. In the meantime, I will try the networking suggestions that she gave me.

Information Technology

1. I decided to order my coffee first since the café was packed with other college students.

2. To remedy this, I vowed to visit the computer store to find the answer, after I finished my coffee.

Paralegal Studies

1. Through the phone, his voice pierced the otherwise quiet office demanding that the legal assistant help him.

2. Sullenly, he murmured a no and terminated the connection.

EXERCISE 2.6: Answers will vary. Paragraphs should be written using narrative form.

Descriptive Writing

EXERCISE 2.7: Answers for this exercise should include the facts using descriptive language. Be certain that you do not add too many adjectives and adverbs.

EXERCISE 2.8:

Allied Health

1, 4, 3, 5, 2, 6

AutoCAD

3, 2, 6, 5, 4, 1

Automotive Technology

5, 1, 2, 4, 3, 6

Criminal Justice

5, 3, 4, 1, 2, 6

Electronics

4, 6, 2, 1, 5, 3

Information Technology

2, 5, 4, 3, 6, 1

Paralegal Studies

3, 1, 6, 4, 5, 2

EXERCISE 2.9: *These are suggested topic sentences that would introduce each of the corresponding paragraphs. Of course, any other response that provides an introduction to the proceeding information is correct.*

Allied Health

Following the three-hour long surgery, the surgical technologist slowly pulled off her gown and gloves, deciding to relax in the lounge.

AutoCAD

The client excitedly introduced his new line of dishes for us to advertise.

Automotive Technology

The task is to check the engine's cooling system for leaks.

Criminal Justice

Proud that I completed most of the obstacle course, I ran as fast as possible towards the last obstacle.

Electronics

Eager to visit his mother, he pushed the doorbell to announce his arrival; nothing sounded.

Information Technology

Okay, let me describe the problem as I understand it.

Paralegal Studies

The client mentioned that he left the papers sitting on the corner of his desk.

EXERCISE 2.10: *For this exercise, be sure that the last sentence concludes the paragraph's information. The supplied endings are suggested conclusions; any sentence that logically completes the paragraph using some description is correct.*

Allied Health

I scheduled an immediate operation for Mrs. Katz; without it, she will die.

AutoCAD

Excitedly, I practiced changing the curve using the other tools, gaining confidence with each new design.

Automotive Technology

With considerable skill in steering, she coaxed the car onto the driveway of the service station.

Criminal Justice

Discouraged by the residents' stubbornness, the officers left the neighborhood.

Electronics

By 3:20 P.M., the rescue crew arrived to take Manual to the hospital.

Information Technology

Angrily, the manager slammed down the phone.

Paralegal Studies

As she opened the door, she signaled to the client to sit in the chair in front of her desk.

EXERCISE 2.11: To answer this exercise effectively, write the topic and concluding sentences to introduce and complete the information given. The following answers represent one set of options. The first sentence in each pair represents the topic sentence with the second representing the conclusion.

Allied Health

1. To make this bathroom safer for Mrs. Acker, add a few safety accessories to the shower.

2. Since she just suffered a debilitating stroke, these accommodations allow her to maintain some independence as she heals.

AutoCAD

1. The client wants to increase the dimensions of the new bedroom by twenty square feet.

2. Once you decide, I can submit a proposed work schedule for you to consider.

Automotive Technology

1. In order to complete all of the work that you want done, I will need another day to work on your car.

2. Thank you for your understanding, I will call you as soon as the work is complete.

Criminal Justice

1. I turned the wide corner, only to have the perpetrator's car race past me on my left, momentarily forcing me off of the road.

2. Finally locating the talk button, I frantically pushed on it to announce the need for assistance from other units.

Electronics

1. I placed the globe onto its platform and then connected the plug to the socket.

2. Excited with the positive test results, I contacted the rest of the team to tell them to begin more globes immediately.

Information Technology

1. Hearing the pops, we scrambled to reach the computer lab room to identify the problem.

2. Our company is debilitated until we can retrieve our customers' account data.

Paralegal Studies

1. Quietly, with headlights turned off, I eased the car into a parking space across from the house.

2. Using my clearest voice, I asked if either man was Mr. Parker.

EXERCISE 2.12: Answers will vary. Paragraphs should be written using descriptive form.

Chapter 3: Logical Connections

<u>Illustrative Writing</u>

EXERCISE 3.1: Answers may vary, but listed below are some suggestions of examples that describe the given word.

Allied Health

1. teeth: incisor, premolar, molar, canine

2. patient care: respite, inpatient, outpatient

3. allied health field: nursing, dental assisting, medical assisting, surgical technology

4. doctor: pediatrician, surgeon, general practitioner, psychiatrist, internist

5. instrument: stethoscope, scalpel, otoscope, percussion hammer, nasal speculum

AutoCAD

1. drawing: 3D rendering, architectural plans, dimensions

2. surface generation: surface extrusion, sweep profile, contour mesh

3. model: 2D models, 3D wireframe, solid frame

4. project: animation project, architectural project, outdoor landscaping design

5. surface properties: face normal, smoothing group, mapping coordinates

Automotive Technology

1. wrench: lug nut wrench, socket wrench, flare nut wrench

2. screwdriver: Torx, Phillips, standard set

3. socket: drive socket set, plug socket, hex socket

4. tires: all-season, run-flat, 80 series

5. car: 4-door, 2-door, sedan, station wagon, sports

Criminal Justice

1. law: state, federal, civil, criminal

2. misdemeanor: first degree, second degree

3. jail: juvenile, adult, county, state, detention center

4. officer: animal control, police, probation, immigration

5. offender: sexual, multiple, first-time

Electronics

1. tools: wire testers, screwdrivers, wire cutters

2. power reader: analog multimeter, digital multimeter, voltmeter

3. electrical charge: positive, negative

4. circuit: parallel circuit, series circuits

5. filters: series resonant, series RLC, parallel RLC

Information Technology

1. computer: laptop, desktop, pocket

2. modem: wireless, external, internal

3. virus: sasser, doomsday, malicious code

4. online connection: dial up, DSL, wireless, cable

5. printer: ink jet, compact, wireless

Paralegal Studies

1. law: real estate, criminal, civil, business

2. criminal charge: larceny, assault, theft

3. civil case: defamation, libel, tort

4. wills: simple, living

5. legal documents: wills, marital dissolutions, titles

EXERCISE 3.2: *Answers for this section will vary. Drawings should include as much detail as possible.*

EXERCISE 3.3: *Responses will vary for this exercise. The most successful ones use specific language to illustrate a point.*

Allied Health

1. His upper left canine throbbed this morning when he awoke.

2. To increase patient satisfaction, we need to spend more time listening to their medical history during intake.

3. In the fall, Mary plans to attend State University to study nursing.

4. After his accident, Jack needed to see his chiropractor, internist, and podiatrist.

5. Please sterilize the speculum so that the doctor can use it with the next patient.

AutoCAD

1. Your 2D plans of the room addition are absolutely perfect for the space!

2. To complete this phase of the animation for the film, add contour mesh to the wireframe model so that the rest of the team can create similar characters.

3. When will the architectural drawings be completed?

4. His wireframe model shows the potential problems with the design; the dimensions need to be modified before the presentation next week.

5. Janet believes that the face normal setting for this model highlights the best features.

Automotive Technology

1. When changing a tire, use a lug nut wrench to loosen lugs on the wheel base.

2. Please pass me the Torx screwdriver that is on the bench behind you.

3. In order for us to replace the oil pan, we need a 3/8-inch socket wrench.

4. The customer requested a set of store brand all-season tires.

5. This morning, Roberto decided to go to the dealership on the corner to purchase a four-door sedan.

Criminal Justice

1. Patricia, arrested for breaking the disorderly conduct statute, refused to stop screaming.

2. Last night, the seventeen-year-old committed a misdemeanor when he refused to return home after the town curfew started.

3. He called from one of the city jails; however, I do not remember which one.

4. As she is completing her studies in criminal justice, she decided to apply to work as a local police officer.

5. Your adult male, sex offender group will meet in the large group room this afternoon.

Electronics

1. Please, bring your ohmmeter with you because the dryer is experiencing power surges during use.

2. Can you use your multimeter to determine where the faulty circuit is located?

3. To test the voltage of each circuit, I need to turn off all of the circuits at the breaker.

4. Check the wire and prongs on the power cord; maybe the connection is loose.

5. The band pass filter allows the signal to travel through the circuit without losing too much amplitude.

Information Technology

1. Marcus wants to buy a new desktop multimedia computer so that he can edit his digital videos with it.

2. The high-speed modem is slower today, particularly in the last hour, than it has been.

3. Beware, the slingbot virus has infected our company's server's boot records.

4. His online connection is much quicker now that he has switched to using a high speed cable service.

5. Maria connected the ink jet printer to the pocket computer even though she has not installed the driver for it.

Paralegal Studies

1. Because of his desire to learn about criminal law, Jason enrolled in college as a paralegal studies major.

2. Her client, despite his protestations, was charged with breaking and entering his own office because he did not have his identification or keys with him when the officer found him inside.

3. Because he refused to fulfill his contract, he must face a civil lawsuit charging him with breech.

4. No one is certain as to whether he left a simple will or whether he died intestate.

5. The subpoenas will be ready for you in the morning by 10:00.

EXERCISE 3.4: Answers for this section will vary. Paragraphs should be written using illustrative form.

Cause and Effect Writing

EXERCISE 3.5: Below are some possible answers for each of the exercises. Use these answers as a guide to examine your writing. Check answers with your instructor to gain the most benefit from these exercises.

Allied Health

effect **1.** Better health care is a result of <u>good preventive care</u>.

effect **2.** All surgical technicians attended the training, meaning <u>they have completed their CEUs for the year</u>.

effect **3.** Dental hygienists must pass a licensing test before they can <u>practice legally</u>.

cause **4.** <u>Three doctors called in sick</u>, which created an overcrowded waiting room.

effect **5.** If you do not floss regularly <u>you contract gingivitis</u>.

cause **6.** <u>Because you have not been taking care of yourself</u>, you have caught a cold.

cause **7.** <u>Whenever he fails to take his medication</u>, he faints.

effect **8.** The board granted two million dollars for the project due to <u>the success of the hospital's research team's project</u>.

effect **9.** Drugs that are stimulants <u>are designed to increase energy</u>.

effect **10.** Untreated high blood pressure <u>can cause heart problems</u>.

AutoCAD

effect **1.** When you slice a solid in half, <u>you are able to work with the diagram shell</u>.

cause **2.** <u>He used the surface toolbar</u>, allowing the designer to see many surfaces at once.

effect **3.** The design team loved her drawings; <u>they have hired her as the lead architect</u>.

effect **4.** Once you have specified the X-axis coordinates, <u>the computer will plot the line</u>.

cause **5.** <u>He pays attention to the small details</u>, which results in a quality design.

cause **6.** <u>When the plans were completed, we noticed that the dimensions of the house did not fit those of the land</u>; that is the purpose for moving the room to the other side of the house.

effect **7.** All of the hours spent studying <u>taught him the value of discipline</u>.

cause **8.** <u>We made all of the requested changes to the plans</u> and now the customer is pleased.

cause **9.** <u>The customer made some changes in his request</u>, which is the reason for the shape of the final product.

effect **10.** Following the procedure for inserting blocks <u>allows for exact placement of all design features</u>.

Automotive Technology

cause **1.** <u>The customer did not use an air pressure gauge when filling the tire</u>, leaving the tire over pressurized.

effect **2.** The calipers were installed upside down meaning <u>the air will never be properly bled from the caliper</u>.

cause **3.** <u>The mechanic installed a faulty part</u>, now the whole steering system must be replaced.

effect **4.** If you do not change your oil regularly, <u>the engine will not last as long</u>.

effect **5.** Worn shock absorbers cause <u>the vehicle to continue to bounce after hitting bumps</u>.

cause **6.** <u>Avoid filling the master cylinder to the top</u> because the fluid overflows when it becomes hot.

cause **7.** <u>Flushing the transmission fluid as directed by the manufacturer</u> results in longer life for the transmission.

effect **8.** It is important to keep the gas tank filled above the quarter tank mark because <u>if it falls below, the car can suffer from rough idle or stalling</u>.

cause **9.** You'll know when a cylinder head gasket has blown because <u>there will be white smoke coming from the tailpipe</u>.

cause **10.** <u>Remember to change the fluid</u> or the brake fluid will boil and cause the brake pedal to go soft.

Criminal Justice

cause **1.** <u>More officers patrolling the streets</u> leads to a decrease in street crime.

effect **2.** The forensic psychologist will write a profile of Jared which <u>will be used during the hearing to prove that he was insane at the time of committing the murder</u>.

effect **3.** Working too many long shifts without taking breaks can cause <u>unhealthy stress reactions</u>.

cause **4.** New victims rights resulted from <u>the increase of publicity in rape cases</u>.

cause **5.** <u>Considering the overcrowding conditions in the city jail</u>, beginning next year, alternative sanctions will be assigned when applicable.

effect **6.** New security measures implemented in airports <u>have increased the safety of all domestic flights</u>.

effect **7.** Community policing is the most effective measure for reducing crime because <u>officers develop community task forces which involve neighbors in the process of keeping their neighborhoods safe</u>.

cause **8.** <u>Troy completes his rehabilitation program soon</u>, meaning that he will leave the detention center next week.

cause **9.** <u>It was discovered that drug use has increased amongst area teens</u>, raising drug crimes significantly.

effect **10.** The school resource officer began an incentive program for students who attend the most classes in a quarter, so far <u>the attendance rates remain unchanged</u>.

Electronics

effect **1.** Due to his hard work on his final electronics project, <u>he earned the highest grade in class</u>.

effect **2.** <u>Ripple voltage</u> is caused by charge and discharge of the capacitor.

cause **3.** <u>He accidently crossed the wires</u> which caused the circuit to short.

effect **4.** Now that the job is complete, <u>the power can be switched back on</u>.

cause **5.** <u>If you follow the schematic</u>, then the components will be properly connected.

effect **6.** <u>Increased energy dissipation</u> is caused by the larger sized resistor.

cause **7.** <u>Failure to change the batteries</u> results in the radio not working.

cause **8.** <u>She discovered a faulty wire in the wall</u>, which explains the occasional dip in power.

cause **9.** <u>The object was removed from its magnetic field</u> so that it loses its magnetic charge.

effect **10.** Inductive reactance causes <u>the total current to lag the source voltage</u>.

Information Technology

cause **1.** <u>The server was offline all morning for systems updates</u>, meaning that no one in the company had access to intranet services.

effect **2.** New spyware detects adware and malicious trojan applications resulting <u>in safer and more efficient web surfing</u>.

effect **3.** Be sure to backup all of your software files or else <u>you are in danger of losing all of your work</u>.

cause **4.** <u>The technician forgot to check for system compatibility when installing the new software package</u> and now the program crashes each time the computer starts up.

cause **5.** <u>The new phone system hardware is installed</u> so the computers can now communicate with the company's phone system.

cause **6.** <u>I was not paying attention when I added email addresses to the message and ended up</u> sending the message to everyone on the general mailing list instead.

effect **7.** He finished installing the wireless system in the café so that <u>customers can access the Internet using their laptops</u>.

effect **8.** If you maintain one customer database, <u>then it is less work to update entries than if you keep multiple ones</u>.

cause **9.** <u>Adding robotic arms to the assembly line</u> increased the productivity in the factory by fifty-percent.

effect **10.** The technology team presented their proposition well this morning, <u>because of this, they should receive funding for the project.</u>

Paralegal Studies

effect **1.** The judge moved up the time of the trial and now <u>we do not have time to prepare for our closing.</u>

effect **2.** The law firm decided to add three more legal assistants to the firm, <u>which will increase billable hours while decreasing workloads of other assistants.</u>

cause **3.** <u>The ruling of Roe vs. Wade focused public attention on the legality of abortion</u> resulting in a change of the abortion laws.

cause **4.** <u>When a parent in a two-parent family dies,</u> the remaining parent retains custody of the minor children.

effect **5.** Long hours of research and study <u>helped him to complete his paralegal degree.</u>

cause **6.** The defense was illogical and not well-researched, which <u>caused a loss sending the client to prison for three years.</u>

cause **7.** <u>The legal assistant discovered new information pertaining to the case,</u> which prompted the attorney to file an appeal.

effect **8.** According to the client, the contractor breached contract leading <u>the attorney to file a civil lawsuit.</u>

cause **9.** <u>The McIntyres failed to pay their mortgage for the third month in a row</u> resulting in foreclosure at the end of the day.

effect **10.** At three o'clock, Roger was served with a subpoena meaning <u>that he will have to appear in court.</u>

EXERCISE 3.6: Responses will vary. All well-written introductory paragraphs will contain a clear statement of the causal relationship with some detail.

EXERCISE 3.7: Responses will vary according to chosen topic. The essays should contain an introductory paragraph followed by two supporting paragraphs and end with a conclusion.

Classification Writing

EXERCISE 3.8:

1. shapes that have flat sides

2. vehicle body styles

3. careers in criminal justice

4. baby mammals

5. secondary colors

6. household tools

7. writing instruments

8. genres of story (book, film)

9. musical styles

10. types of tables

EXERCISE 3.9: Responses will vary; however, most will be close to the sentences below.

Allied Health

1. There are two types of manometers used to measure blood pressure: aneroid and mercury.

2. To safely practice universal precautions, use items designed for safety such as masks and latex gloves when treating every patient.

AutoCAD

1. Dash and long-dash dot are line types that can be used with the drawing.

2. There are two methods to use for changing dimension text: DIMEDIT and DIMTEDIT.

Automotive

1. Two methods used for discovering the source of electrical problems are fuse replacement and circuit breaker.

2. Most vehicles use either V4 or V8 engines for power.

Criminal Justice

1. There are two types of imprisonments utilized in prisons today: selective and collective incapacitation.

2. Courts, such as community or federal, exist as a means to mete out punishments to offenders or to dismiss the innocent.

Electronics

1. There are two types of multimeters: analog and digital.

2. When choosing a circuit, you must choose the kind that fits the job best, for example, series or parallel.

Information Technology

1. There are a couple of methods available for increasing the speed of your computer: use of greater chip density and installation of an accelerator board.

2. Two types of infrastructure providers are network and component.

Paralegal Studies

1. A summons and a complaint/original petition are documents that are commonly used in a simple civil action.

2. Marriage licenses and birth certificates are state issued documents used as proof of notation in public record.

EXERCISE 3.10: Responses will vary according to chosen topic. The essays should begin with one of the sentences written in EXERCISE 3.9. Paragraphs should contain at least five sentences that are used to describe the common grouping/classification of the items introduced.

EXERCISE 3.11: Responses will vary according to chosen topic. The essays should contain at least five paragraphs: introduction, three descriptive paragraphs with supporting detail, and a conclusion.

Comparison-Contrast Writing

EXERCISE 3.12: Check your answers with the given example. Use the sample answers as a guide.

Allied Health

Topic A
Working in a doctor's/dentist's office vs. Working in a hospital

Similarities	Differences
both are in the medical fields	private offices have set hours/hospitals don't
pay is approximately the same	more opportunity for promotion in a hospital

Topic B
Working as a per diem employee vs. Working as a fixed shift employee

Similarities	Differences
can earn a living working for either	per diem allows for more hours
can work the same amount of hours	fixed shift employees are guaranteed work

AutoCAD

Topic A

2D Drawing vs. 3D Rendering

Similarities	Differences
both are used to change an image	2D images are transparent/profiles
both are used to create models	3D images show the finished product

Topic B

Working for a company, agency, or business vs. Working as a contractor

Similarities	Differences
both pay approximately the same	contractors set own work hours
both require the same job functions	more employment stability with agency

Automotive Technology

Topic A

V4 engines vs. V8 engines

Similarities	Differences
both can power cars	V4 engines use less gasoline
both are similar in build	V8 can power a heavier vehicle

Topic B

Manual transmission vs. Automatic transmission

Similarities	Differences
both are used to regulate speed	manuals use two pedals
both work the same inside the engine	automatics do not require gear shifting

Criminal Justice

Topic A

Working for a security company vs. Working for the police force

Similarities	Differences
both offer approximately same pay	police work in various settings
both require same job function	security: more flexibility in scheduling

Topic B

Jails vs. Prisons

Similarities	Differences
same general work environment	prisons hold criminals for longer time
pay is approximately the same	jails offer fewer rehabilitation services

Electronics

Topic A

AC power vs. DC power

Similarities	Differences
both are used to power households	DC creates power from ac current
both can exist in practical circuits	AC reverses direction in response to polarity

Topic B

Electrical contracting vs. Working as a lineman

Similarities	Differences
both earn approximately the same pay	contractors set own hours
both use the same general knowledge	linemen work is steadier

Information Technology

Topic A

Windows vs. Macintosh

Similarities	Differences
both are operating systems	Macintosh: used for complex multimedia
both function the same, in general	Windows programs are cheaper

Topic B

Dial-up Internet vs. DSL Internet

Similarities	Differences
both serve the same purpose	dial up service is cheaper
both are used in homes	DSL connections are quicker

Paralegal Studies

Topic A

Real estate law vs. Criminal law

Similarities	Differences
both require specific training	real estate is a civil discipline
both are specialties of law	criminal law requires more research

Topic B

Working in a small law firm vs. Working in a large law firm

Similarities	Differences
both require the same job knowledge	more opportunity for promotion: large firm
both offer full-time hours	better opportunity to learn: small firm

EXERCISE 3.13: Sentences will differ according to answers in Exercise 3.12. Check that the sentences introduce the topic and list some of the similarities. Look for the use of transitions that strengthen the connections.

EXERCISE 3.14: Sentences will differ according to answers in Exercise 3.12. Check that the sentences introduce the contrast and list some examples. Look for transitions that emphasize the differences.

EXERCISE 3.15: When correcting these essays, consider the structure and details used. The best essays contain logical point-by-point connections using transitions.

EXERCISE 3.16: Essays should clearly follow one of the two organizational structures. It would be best to identify the style used.

Process Writing

EXERCISE 3.17: Since responses will vary, use the answers below as a guide. If your answers are similar, then you are writing the style properly.

Allied Health

Process: Sterilizing instruments before use

List of materials needed: instrument to be sterilized, cold water, hot water, soap, stiff bristled brush, sterile towel, and basin

AutoCAD

Process: Creating a scene for a model

List of materials needed: computer, AutoCAD program, chosen lighting effects, chosen view, chosen background picture

Automotive Technology:

Process: Changing a tire on a car

List of materials needed: car, flat tire, jack, lug nut wrench, flat surface to work

Criminal Justice

Process: Arresting an offender

List of materials needed: offender, cause for arrest, handcuffs, and Miranda rights

Electronics

Process: Reading a digital multimeter

List of materials needed: circuit to be measured, test wires, alligator clips, digital multimeter

Information Technology

Process: Burning a CD

List of materials needed: blank CD, a CD-RW drive (external or internal), computer, information to transfer to disk

Paralegal Studies

Process: Filing for a dissolution of marriage

List of materials needed: fulfillment of the residency requirement, documentation of date and place of marriage, statement that the marriage is irrevocably broken, proof of names and ages of each minor child, request for wife's restoration of maiden name, and property settlement agreement

EXERCISE 3.18: Responses for this section will differ; use this information as a guide to check format. The sentences should include a topic sentence and a reference to the materials needed to complete the task, event, or situation.

Allied Health

Process: Sterilizing instruments before use

Introduction: It is essential that you learn to sterilize your instruments before using them on a patient. Before beginning, assemble all of the following items: instrument to be sterilized, cold water, hot water, soap, stiff bristled brush, sterile towel, and basin.

AutoCAD

Process: Creating a scene for a model

Introduction: Once you have designed your model, you will want to create a scene that will display it. Before you begin this task, gather all needed supplies such as a computer, AutoCAD program, chosen lighting effects, chosen view, and chosen background picture.

Automotive Technology

Process: Changing a flat tire

Introduction: There is nothing more frustrating than experiencing a flat tire, especially when in a rush. To change the flat, it is important to be sure that you have the needed tools before beginning: car, flat tire, jack, lug nut wrench, and a flat surface to work.

Criminal Justice

Process: Arresting an offender

Introduction: Officers must follow procedures when arresting an offender. It is important that before attempting to arrest the offender, you have ascertained that there is enough evidence to do so.

Electronics

Process: Reading a digital multimeter

Introduction: Digital multimeters measure ohms, DC and AC voltage, and current. Before reading the multimeter, be sure that you have wires and alligator clips.

Information Technology

Process: Burning a CD

Introduction: With new technology, information is saved, including music, on CDs through the process of burning. Before burning a CD, you will need an internal or external CD burner along with a writable CD.

Paralegal Studies

Process: Dissolution of a marriage

Introduction: Before a couple can file for dissolution of marriage, proof of legal status of a few conditions must be met. The law stipulates that the couple must supply the court with documents showing proof of residency, proof of legal marriage, birth dates and names of minor children, and a property distribution agreement before a dissolution hearing is scheduled.

EXERCISE 3.19: The steps for this exercise can be listed in numerical order or can be written in a paragraph showing the steps in order. Whichever format is used is fine, the key to this exercise is the challenge of arranging steps in logical order. There are no suggested processes given because it is important to choose a topic that you know well.

EXERCISE 3.20: Responses may vary, but below are some sample answers.

Allied Health

1. Chart a patient's progress.
    To chart a patient's progress, be sure that you have measured his/her vital signs before beginning to write.

2. Check a patient's blood pressure.
    To read a patient's blood pressure accurately, be sure that the cuff is functional and positioned correctly.

3. Use universal precautions when working with all patients.
    When working with patients, use universal precautions such as wearing tight fitting, latex gloves.

AutoCAD

1. Render a figure.
    Before rendering an image, check your dimensions with your needs.

2. Add a gradient to the design, so that it matches that of the yard.
    To add a gradient to a design, survey the yard for slopes and dips, once you have done this, you can add a proportionate gradient to your plans.

3. Animate the buttons of the webpage.
    Once the basic web page is created, decide which buttons will be animated.

Automotive Technology

1. Change the oil in the car.
    To change the oil in a car, be sure that you have the proper kind of oil available.

2. Check the charge in a car battery.
    The first step in checking the charge in a car that has just been driven is to remove the surface charge.

3. Check the air pressure in the tires.
    Before testing the pressure in your tires, be sure that your pressure gauge is giving accurate readings.

Criminal Justice

1. Write an arrest report.
    In order to write an arrest report, be sure that you have gathered all of the facts first, otherwise, you will have to revise it later.

2. Dust a door for fingerprints.
    Dust the door for fingerprints first, because this is a high traffic area; it is too easy for someone to touch the door frame without realizing it.

3. Write an abuse report.
    So, after making certain that a report is to be filed, write down all of the facts so that they are in front of you when you call the state abuse hotline.

266

Electronics

1. Check the ground of a wire.
   It is essential that you check the ground of active wires before attempting to work with them.

2. Test a circuit breaker for power.
   Before changing any of the circuit breaker positions, make note of which switches are on and which are off.

3. Measure the input voltage response.
   Use a multimeter to check the input voltage response.

Information Technology

1. Check for a modem connection.
   Check the wire connections between the computer and the phone jack.

2. Install a software program.
   Place the CD containing the software program into the CD ROM drive.

3. Print a document.
   Open the document that you want to be printed and select print from the file menu.

Paralegal Studies

1. Write a closing statement for a house.
   To write a closing statement for a house, you will need all of the preliminary documents showing the owner's and buyer's information.

2. Prepare a complaint.
   Before writing the complaint, be sure that you have gathered all of the facts involved.

3. Research a case using law books.
   When preparing to conduct research using law books, be sure that you know the facts of the current case so that your work will be easier.

EXERCISE 3.21: Essays should contain a topic sentence which introduces the process to be followed and a list of materials or information needed. The rest of the essay should contain detailed steps that guide the reader.

Chapter 4-Persuasion

<u>Persuasive Writing</u>

***EXERCISE 1**: Answers should provide support to the opening statement thereby persuading the reader to consider an opinion. Consider these answers to be examples.*

Allied Health

1. Last night the medical assistants decided to strike in response to the rumor of impending salary reductions.

AutoCAD

1. To earn the most money for this project, we will have to work late hours and reduce our overhead.

Automotive

1. I think that the transmission should be flushed now because the engine is not performing efficiently and the fluid is dirty.

Criminal Justice

1. Terrorism threats remain high now because according to the intelligence reports, there is increased chatter from the Middle East.

Electronics

1. To properly install a circuit breaker, one must first turn off the power to that circuit so that there is not a risk of electrocution.

Information Technology

1. In my opinion, laptops are better computers than desktops because many jobs require mobility; laptops can be used virtually anywhere.

Paralegal Studies

1. I think that all legal assistants and secretaries in our office earned a raise this quarter because each of them worked tirelessly on our biggest case allowing us to win a large settlement.

***EXERCISES 4.2–4.5**: Answers to these questions should include a logical response to the prompt. Responses will vary.*

Argumentative Writing

Allied Health

1. It is unfair to require medical assistants to work twelve-hour shifts because <u>they have not had a break during that time.</u>

2. Staff nurses earn less money per shift than pool nurses do. I believe that this is wrong because <u>unlike per diem nurses, they are guaranteed work.</u>

3. When the new wing of the clinic opens, patients who cannot pay for service will not be treated. This wrong in my opinion <u>because according to our Hippocratic oath, we should do no harm and turning away needy patients can potentially harm them.</u>

4. Hospital policy states that all medical personnel must attend training in HIPAA annually; I think that this is a waste of time since <u>HIPAA regulations do not change yearly and allows for protection of patient rights.</u>

5. In our office, senior staff members are promoted over junior ones despite qualifications. I do not think that this is fair because <u>the promoted person is not always the best for the job.</u>

AutoCAD

1. To save money, most of the studio's animators should be fired because <u>too often, there are two or more animators working to create the same character.</u>

2. Company policy dictates that all engineers must use their computers when working on client designs. This policy is a bad one because <u>sometimes an engineer may feel inspired to work from home.</u>

3. In my opinion, the AutoCAD program at our school is one of the best due to <u>its ability to revise backgrounds and gradients easily.</u>

4. Though the team opted to use a foggy background setting for the storyboard, I disagreed because <u>the fog obscures the details of the characters.</u>

5. Our proposal to update the computer system was denied because there is not enough money in the budget to support the proposed upgrades, but this is a short sighted decision due to <u>the vulnerability of our current system.</u>

Automotive Technology

1. Even though car manufacturers suggest an engine oil change every 5,000 miles, it is better to change it every 3,000 because <u>your engine performs best with fresh oil</u>.

2. Some new cars include DVD players below the rearview mirror, but this is a dangerous trend <u>because drivers may pay attention to the movie rather than to the road</u>.

3. The new policy of preventing customers from watching the mechanic work on their cars is wrong <u>because some customers want to monitor the work</u>.

4. The practice of replacing worn parts with used parts is not always a good one because <u>sometimes the old parts do not match the vehicle exactly</u>.

5. Some shops hire mechanics that have not passed their certification tests, but this practice is still a practical one since <u>mechanics can train with master mechanics</u>.

Criminal Justice

1. Capitol punishment is necessary as a deterrent to crime because <u>death is the only punishment that some people fear</u>.

2. To reduce cruelty to animals, penalties must <u>be given to offenders</u>.

3. I believe that all juveniles who commit crimes should <u>be enrolled in behavior modification programs and counseling</u>.

4. Impounded vehicles should be sold at auctions <u>to help pay for fees accrued</u>.

5. All those convicted of drug charges should serve strict jail sentences because <u>they will learn that the penalties for breaking drug laws is worse than using drugs</u>.

Electronics

1. To generate more energy, wind power should be harnessed rather than building more nuclear plants <u>as this will reduce pollution</u>.

2. Tree limbs should be cut away from power lines before the arrival of the storm season <u>because they present a risk to houses</u>.

3. Everyone should take advantage of energy conservation programs offered by electric companies because <u>it is our responsibility to save earth's resources</u>.

4. All linemen should be required to attend safety procedures training annually <u>due to the increased number of accidents that occurred on the job last year</u>.

5. In my opinion, our electronics program at school is one of the best because <u>instructors spend time working individually with students</u>.

Information Technology

1. I believe that we should invest in the most expensive server that we can afford because <u>it will not require updating as frequently as a cheaper server</u>.

2. Some software companies monopolize the market using unfair tactics; to me, this is wrong <u>because when one company creates all the products, prices go up</u>.

3. Websites that allow people to exchange music files are <u>great since no one has to pay for the music</u>.

4. Computer hackers who break into a system with a non-malicious virus must be <u>prosecuted for tampering with the property of others</u>.

5. In my opinion, our Information Technology program at school is better than yours because <u>our instructors work with us individually and yours do not</u>.

Paralegal Studies

1. I disagree with our firm's policy of requiring legal assistants to work overtime during certain times of the year because <u>some of them cannot work during those times</u>.

2. According to our state law, legal assistants can perform only some duties without supervision of a lawyer. They should be allowed to do more <u>so that law firms can bill for more hours</u>.

3. I believe that capitol punishment does not deter people from committing crimes <u>because they do not seem to care about the consequences of their actions</u>.

4. Illegal immigrants who have resided in the United States for a period of five years should be given legal status because <u>they have managed to live in the country as citizens</u>.

5. The Paralegal Studies program at our school is better than yours because <u>we spend six months working as interns in law firms</u>.

EXERCISE 4.7: Answers will vary for this section. The best answers contain both a clear position and support of the position.

EXERCISE 4.8: Answers will vary for this section. The best answers state the position and support it using detail.

Review of the Nine Writing Styles

1. narrative

   Characteristics: use of first person, described the events chronologically

2. classification

   Characteristics: lists a general category and sub-categories

3. persuasive

   Characteristics: states an opinion/point of view

4. cause and effect

   Characteristics: presents a condition followed by a direct effect

5. comparison/contrast

   Characteristics: presents a choice and then gives pros and cons

6. illustrative

   Characteristics: describes an example

7. argumentative

   Characteristics: presents a case and supportive detail

8. descriptive

   Characteristics: uses sense words to describe a scene

9. process

   Characteristics: introduces a "how to" for beginning a job search

PART III: Punctuation
Chapter 5: Simple Punctuation

COMMAS

EXERCISE 5.1:

1. The client's attorney, the client, the defendant's attorney, and the defendant met in a room at the courthouse to file a deposition.

2. To assist the client, the legal assistant prepared questions to be used during the deposition.

3. The medical insurance claim information is to be sent to 2635 Westerly Ave. Memphis, Tennessee by tomorrow morning.

4. Shelia, Marty, and Thomas need to select backgrounds and wipes to complete their animation project.

5. With circuits overloaded, the team of electricians worked to create an alternative wiring plan.

6. Yesterday, the managers met with the technology committee to discuss the timeline of the system upgrades, the allocation of funds, and possible locations for the new server.

7. The manager, John Dorsey, will start work in the garage this morning.

8. His work in the operating room is a meticulous, efficient example for all medical students to follow.

9. "From this draft, you are to create a 3-D rendering so that we can begin production in few days," the supervisor directed.

10. Mechanics learn how to diagnose, fix, and perform preventive maintenance on engines while training to take the certification test sponsored by the National Institute for Automotive Service Excellence.

11. After, we will use the resistor to test the voltage given by the motor.

12. The probation officer stated, "I met with the probationer on Monday morning, before noon, for his scheduled appointment. We scheduled another appointment for the same time next month."

13. However, the licensing agreement reads that the program can be installed on three separate home computers.

14. No such law has been enacted in the past two hundred years and yet, it is unclear as to why.

15. Ms. Dartmouth, the medical assistant, is not able to cover the third shift tonight.

16. In this drawing, you need to take information from a three-dimensional perspective and develop it into a 3view instead.

17. Therefore, an open or break anywhere in the control circuit will prevent the operation of the starter motor.

18. Officer McHaley, the officer on duty, can answer your questions.

19. The advanced electronics exam is a long, difficult test suitable for those who are close to graduating this semester.

20. Not all software written for that system is inefficient, however.

21. Penal Law 1053 states that, "Any person, who while engaged in hunting, shall discharge a firearm or operate a long bow in a culpably negligent manner is guilty of criminal negligence while engaged in hunting."

22. The doctor asked the nurse to take the medical history, check the blood pressure, and give a flu shot to the patient in room four.

23. Thus, when the inductance is increased the opposition to current increases.

24. In this exercise, we will practice scaling the text and lines that you completed drawing previously.

25. The store processor is a file server for the cash registers, providing product and pricing information, while capturing the customer's purchasing preferences.

26. Suppose, for example, that you are unable to find the references that you need in the law library, then you can use this online database.

27. "I need my car fixed no later than 4:00 P.M. this afternoon because I have a meeting," implored the customer.

28. Fluoride can be given to patients topically, through the water system, and through vitamin supplements.

29. First, create the image that you want to develop and then decide on the dimensions.

30. Jayne, fast-talking and bright, managed to elude police for years before being captured today.

31. The Eastshore Electric Company, the new area utility provider, will lower power rates for all customers.

32. Ms. Jackson directed, "Place the new computers in the back of the room so that we can set up each one individually."

33. The width of the grooves, the width of the lands between the ring grooves, and the number of the rings are major factors in determining minimum piston height.

34. Tomorrow, I graduate with my Associate's degree in electronic technology.

35. Dr. Parker, the new physician on staff, will be giving a talk tomorrow for all medical assistants.

36. Talented, hard-working students are hired by that firm every summer.

37. Vapor lock is caused by bubbles that form in the fuel preventing proper operation of the fuel pump, carburetor, or fuel-injection system.

38. The Internet computer networks, business servers, and automated data systems present many new opportunities for committing criminal activity.

39. "I believe that the heating element in the water heater needs replacing," she reported.

40. The problem is that in order to install, run, and test the antivirus software the entire system will be shut down for an hour

41. This case, exciting yet challenging, is quite time consuming.

42. For absorption to occur, the correct form of the drug must be given by the route intended.

43. The complex symbol is the completed, fully detailed model.

44. To cause inflation, the closing of the arming sensor is required to provide the power-side voltage to the inflator module.

45. "You need to stay seated until we come for you," the officer told the detainee.

46. Also, the period can be measured from any peak in a given cycle to the corresponding peak in the next cycle.

47. DSL is always operational, meaning that the channel is active at all times.

48. Since no contract exists, the recipient is under no obligation to either pay the merchant or return the item.

49. "Sit back in the chair and close your eyes to relax while you wait for the dentist," the hygienist recommended.

50. The customer, the man in the orange shirt sitting in the corner, requested a word with the mechanic.

51. "Your performance this month was exceptional," his supervisor reported.

52. The secondary winding is connected to the circuit containing the rectifier filter, terminal, and regulator.

53. The new laptops, slimmer and quicker than the older models, will revolutionize our industry.

54. The case files, the ones that you requested, are sitting in the warehouse waiting for delivery.

55. Yesterday, I discovered that the local pharmacy has openings for full-time technicians.

56. "I met with the customer an hour ago," I began before being interrupted by the ringing of the phone.

57. There is also the danger of freezing when a battery is discharged, because the electrolyte is mostly water.

58. The agent, the one that uncovered the smuggling ring, was promoted this morning.

59. Five transport technologies are in widespread use, including (1) frame delay, (2) ATM, (3) DSL, (4) ISDN, (5) SMDS.

60. Those expenses might include the difference between the contract price and the going rate of the open market, lost profits, replacement or completion costs, or other amounts.

61. Writing new programs, ones that increase line productivity, is both time consuming and lucrative.

62. Next, check the patient's cholesterol so that we have all of the necessary information to make the diagnosis.

63. The architect will meet you on Tuesday, October 30 at 3:00 P.M.

64. "Check the oil gasket, oil tray, and oil level because the customer is worried that there may be a leak," Jake told the mechanic.

65. Correctional officers, who are well trained, often work in dangerous conditions.

66. When two like poles are brought close together, they repel each other.

67. Be sure that when you purchase your new computer that you also purchase cables, a printer, and system software.

68. A legal assistant is prohibited, of course, from rendering legal advice in either situation although the attendance of the paralegal at these events is not generally a problem.

69. Touch, cuddling, visual, and auditory stimulation are all-critical for the infant.

70. Keep in mind, however, that using too small a lens length can greatly distort the display of the model.

71. The mid-size car of the year, the one that most consumers bought, is the one that needs the least repairs.

72. Recently, the city police attempted to disrupt gang activity by passing a city ordinance prohibiting public loitering in front of local businesses.

73. Please meet the other linemen on Wednesday, June 1 at the regional office for the annual safety training.

74. The use of instant messages on the Internet, a sort of combination of real-time chat and e-mail, has grown rapidly since it was introduced in the late 1990s.

75. "Prepare the briefs according to the format discussed in class," the professor said as he gave the assignment.

76. When patients fail to floss, they develop more cavities.

77. This method of drawing circles is almost the same as the radius method, except you do not use the default and you will see that the rubber band works differently.

78. Resistors, as well as other components, should be operated substantially below their rated values to enhance their reliability.

79. The computer may, therefore, need to scan several hundred feet of tape to find the record you want.

80. Also, one party may act as the primary custodial parent while both parties share parental responsibilities on issues such as religion, schooling, medical treatment, and other matters.

81. "So, your next appointment is scheduled for our new office located on 364 High Street, behind the new strip mall," the receptionist informed the patient.

82. To use it, you need to specify the present orientation of the object relative to the coordinate system.

83. This type of master cylinder is also called dual-diameter, bore step-bore, or fast-fill master cylinder.

84. In some cases, after isolating a fault to a particular circuit, it may be necessary to isolate the problem to a single component in the circuit.

85. The Small Business Administration, a branch of the United States government, was created to assist small-business owners.

86. Terrorism, as a criminal activity, and the prevention of further acts of terrorism became primary concerns of the government following the attacks of September 11, 2001.

87. When the contract offer was originally made, the buyer gave the seller until 5:00 P.M. on May 16, 2004 to accept.

88. Vitamin D, which is largely derived from sunshine, is instrumental in balancing the calcium and phosphorus ratio in the body.

89. The Shell suboption creates a hollow, thin wall with a specified thickness.

90. Determine if there is a fault and if so, identify it.

91. This idea stresses that in general, IT works best when it adjusts to people, not when people have to adjust to it.

92. "Have a seat, the attorney will be with you in a moment," replied the receptionist to the client.

93. Appointment control will prevent overcrowding, keep hours within desired limits, organize the dentist's production time, assign tasks to the proper individual, and provide patients with definite appointment times.

94. The draft, left on the table, is the one that he needed for this morning's meeting.

95. Next, check the circuit breaker, usually located on the fuse panel, using a test light.

96. The electrician is scheduled to check the system next week, Thursday, August 14, at 2:00 P.M.

97. The system upgrade is efficient, fast, and will save your technicians countless hours.

98. In light of the discussion, it should be clear that depending on the legal issues involved, he will be found innocent.

99. Medical assistants, surgical technicians, and nurses will attend the same orientation on Tuesday.

100. Sean boasted, "What did the client think of our presentation yesterday? Our drawings were definitely the best there."

END PUNCTUATION

EXERCISE 5.2:

1. Late last night, the officer spotted three men breaking into the bank.

2. What do you think is the best method for determining the value of the equivalent resistance of the input circuit?

3. When the victim reported to the precinct, he was still in shock from witnessing the murder.

4. Beware of the sasser worm; it will destroy your hard drive!

5. Walking home from work, it occurred to me that I left the deposition papers on my desk; could you bring them with you when you come?

6. What do you mean that Jane quit? We have to replace her immediately.

7. Working late at night can be hazardous to your health.

8. Use caution when connecting jumper cables to battery terminals on a car; they might explode if the connection is wrong.

9. Do you know when they are going to add more dental hygienists to the staff?

10. The client liked our drawings. That is the best news that I have heard in ages!

11. Call 9-1-1, a lineman has been struck by lightening!

12. To ensure proper care, bathe the wound twice daily and replace the dressing.

13. Do we want to use a wireframe or surface model with these drafts?

14. How he conducts his operating room is strictly his choice.

15. Route the wires over the door so that no one will trip on the cables.

16. Many feel that the law is unconstitutional; what are your feelings about it?

17. Given the treatment options, she is afraid of choosing the wrong one.

18. I need help right away! My car broke down on a remote highway.

19. Which do you prefer: to serve five years of probation or one year in jail?

20. We are planning a career fair for next week. Are you interested in participating?

APOSTROPHES

EXERCISE 5.3:

1. While in the operating room, the surgical technologist couldn't answer her phone.

2. Yesterday, the engineer completed his plans for the project and now he's waiting for approval from the client to begin construction.

3. Did you try to loosen the lug nuts because the customer said that he wasn't able to get them to budge?

4. He left his tools at the last customer's house; he'll have to return to retrieve them.

5. To create the client's webpage, the web designer asked for a meeting with the design team to gather their opinions.

6. Are you sure she's willing to participate in the research study? Let me know if she won't.

7. After everyone left last night, I wasn't able to concentrate on the research for the case, so I left for home instead.

8. Does anyone know its origin? I am certain that I should've known that.

9. Sometimes, it's stressful to work in our office especially during the flu season when we can't see everyone who walks into the clinic.

10. I didn't understand yesterday's lesson about creating chamfers and fillets on solid objects though I stayed up all night trying.

11. I've discovered that if I start the engine without pumping the gas, the motor seems sluggish; can you please take a look at it?

12. He wasn't able to check the resistance because the coil isn't large enough.

13. Like stress, fatigue can affect a police officer's performance.

14. The computer user's desktop is not working properly; it's not showing all of the startup icons.

15. Wouldn't it better if you considered filing a claim against him?

16. For now, I'm considering working as a per diem home health care worker instead of working full time for one home. What do you think about that?

17. The belt's squealing indicates a problem that should be addressed immediately.

18. I left a copy of my resume and a cover letter with him yesterday even though he said that they're not hiring anyone presently.

19. The images lines seem rough to me, aren't you able to smooth them?

20. She's going to intern in the fall with the department though she can't spend a full day with the officer. She'll still earn her required hours.

Chapter 6: Advanced Punctuation

SEMICOLONS

EXERCISE 6.1:

1. Various kinds of permissible activities require the paralegal to use legal judgment; as long as the attorney reviews and approves the documents prior to sending them, the attorney takes responsibility.

2. Many formulas exist for assessing reading levels of written material; nurses involved in developing written health teaching materials should write for lower levels.

3. Basic to the conflict perspective is the belief that the conflict is a fundamental aspect of social life; at best, according to this perspective, formal agencies of society control the unempowered to comply with the rules.

4. A starter solenoid is an electromagnetic switch containing two separate, but connected, electromagnetic windings; this switch is used to engage the starter drive and control the current from the battery to the starter motor.

5. Digestion begins in the oral cavity; the enzyme ptyalin begins the digestion of starch and lubricates the food bolus.

6. When inserting a 3D model, it is important to orient the model; this orientation usually is controlled by the current model's presently active UCS working plane.

7. When resistors are connected in the parallel, the current has more than one path; the number of current paths is equal to the number of parallel branches.

8. The universal serial bus (USB) is one of the most recent additions to PC's; it was created as a general-purpose port that can connect up to 128 devices, all using the same connector.

9. Data communication is an integral component of information technology and many computing applications records of text and data in a job database can include, for example, employee information including name, date hired, and job title as in this individual record; Sally Thomas, August 2, 1988, Customer service representative; Morgan Farris, May 4, 1991, Advertising director; Bert Render, March 2, 1976, Marketing manager; and Earl James, February 5, 1982, Quality control supervisor.

10. The usefulness of Thevenin's theorem can be illustrated when it is applied to a Wheatstone bridge circuit; for example, consider the case when a load resistor is connected to the output terminals of a Wheatstone Bridge.

11. An interactive method for displaying a view of the model can be accomplished by using the 3DORBIT command; you can access the command by typing it on the command line, picking it from the View pull-down menu, or using the 3D Orbit icon.

12. Congenital refers to a condition that exists at or before birth; some common congenital defects of the oral cavity are missing teeth, cleft palate, and many facial defects.

13. An AC generator generates an alternating current when the current changes polarity during the generator's rotation; however, a battery cannot "store" alternating current.

14. Procedural law is another kind of statutory law; it is a body of rules that regulates the processing of an offender by the criminal justice system.

15. Roger Gould theorizes the natural progression of life that marks the path to adult maturity: from ages 16 to 18; ages 18 to 22; ages 22 to 28; ages 29 to 34; ages 35 to 43; ages 43 to 50; ages 50 to 60.

16. Attorneys are responsible for the actions of their employees in both malpractice and disciplinary proceedings; in the vast majority of the cases, the courts have not censured the attorneys for the particular act delegated to the legal assistant.

17. The drafting of legal documents in the absence of the attorney is not per se a violation of ethical standards; the drafting process is not considered unsupervised as long as the attorney gives the work a stamp of approval before the client sees it.

18. Both the client and the nurse should evaluate the learning experience; the client may tell the nurse what was helpful, interesting, and so on.

19. Most private security firms today depend on their own training programs to prevent actionable mistakes by their employees; training in private security operations is also available from a number of schools and agencies.

20. All major battery manufacturers stamp codes on the battery case that give the date of manufacture and other information; most battery manufacturers use a number to indicate the year of manufacture and a letter to indicate month of manufacture.

21. Some developmental pathologic conditions that affect the teeth include anodontia, a lack of development of the teeth; supernumerary teeth, an excess number of teeth; microdontia, teeth that are small in size; and macrodontia, teeth that are large in size.

22. Exterior lighting is controlled by the headlight switch, which is connected directly to the battery on most vehicles; therefore, if lights are left on, it can drain the battery.

23. Vehicles present a special law enforcement problem; they are highly mobile, and when a driver is arrested, the need to search the vehicle may be immediate.

24. The term psychologic homeostasis refers to emotional or psychologic balance or a state of mental well-being; it is maintained by a variety of mechanisms.

25. Shepard's Citations verify the current status of a known case, rule, or law; for example, numbers in a Shepard Citation might look like: Part 1, page 701; Part 4, page 602; Part 17, page 411.

COLONS

EXERCISE 6.2:

1. Paralegals are often asked to "brief" cases: a short summary of a case with its primary points of law organized into a certain format.

2. The nursing process involves five major steps: assess, diagnose, plan, implement, and evaluate.

3. Misdemeanors are relatively minor crimes consisting of offenses such as petty theft, simple assault, breaking and entering, possession of burglary tools, disorderly conduct, and disturbing the peace.

4. Airbags are known by many different names: supplemental restraint system, supplemental inflatable restraints, supplemental air restraints.

5. There are several different ways to administer drugs: orally, inhalation, topically, sublingually, injection, intravenous, and intramuscular.

6. The VPOINT commands contain four methods of entering a location including: entering the three-dimensional, X Y Z coordinates, rotating the model through angles, rotating the model by use of a compass, and using preset locations.

7. When a circuit has more than one resistor of the same value in a series, there is a shortcut method to obtain the total resistance: simply multiply the resistance value of the resistors having the same value by the number of equal-value resistors that are in a series.

8. In the 1990s, second generation digital access technologies were introduced: TDMA, CDMA, and GSM.

9. Representative examples of horizontal exchanges include: IMARK.com, Employease, MRO.com. BidCom, and YOUtilities.

10. The basic categories of voltmeters include the following: electromagnetic, analog voltmeter, and digital voltmeter.

11. Command entry into AutoCAD can be accomplished in several ways: using the command line through the keyboard, a pull down menu, a cursor context menu, a tool from the toolbar, a tablet menu, and a button menu.

12. The periodontium consists of those tissues that support tooth function including: the gingival, alveolar bone, periodontal ligament, and cementum.

13. Older vehicles used a system to control evaporator pressure when used with a continually-operating compressor including: a POA valve and an EPR valve.

14. Our legal system generally recognizes four broad categories of defenses: alibis, justifications, excuses, and procedural defenses.

15. To implement the care plan successfully, nurses need special skills: cognitive, interpersonal, and technical.

16. The court bailiff has many duties including: being responsible for assisting the court in maintaining order, custody of the prisoner while in court, and custody of the jurors.

17. The citation contains the location where the case may be found in the law library as well as other pertinent information: the court, the district in which it was heard, and the year of decision.

18. Several positions are frequently required during physical assessment: dorsal recumbent, horizontal recumbent, sitting, lithonomy, Sims', and prone.

19. One important measure of police success is strongly linked to citizen satisfaction: response time.

20. All electrical circuits require three things to operate: a voltage source, an electrical load, and a ground connection.

21. When cementing temporary crowns, the consistency and amount of cement placed in the temporary crown depends on one thing: the type of crown to be seated.

22. Axonometric viewing makes use of orthographic techniques: to view an object commonly known as parallel projection.

23. The unbalanced bridge is used to measure several types of physical quantities: mechanical strain, temperature, or pressure.

24. Today's portals offer several functions: search capability, access to specialized functions, personalization of content, and communities of interest.

25. The three endodontic instruments used in root canals are: files, broaches, and reamers.

DASHES AND PARENTHESES

EXERCISE 6.3:

1. The screw jack assembly (sometimes called the gear nut) is used to move the front or back of the seat cushion up and down.

2. Use the pen grasp for hand instruments—explorers and spoon excavators.

3. The five goals of sentencing (retribution, incapacitation, deterrence, rehabilitation, restoration) represent a quasi-independent sentencing philosophy.

4. The wireless technology (for cellular communications service) transmits radio messages between a mobile device such as a mobile telephone, PDA, or wireless laptop and a cell site.

5. By observing the direction of the icon arrowhead, you can easily tell which way the X and Y axes are pointing (see figure 4.6).

6. A nurse may require assistance because he/she is unable to implement the nursing activity safely on his or her own—ambulating an unsteady obese client.

7. Points of law drawn from the case by the publisher (called headnotes) are important tools in helping the reader gain an insight into the contents of the case.

8. A radian (rad) is the angle formed when the distance along the circumference of a circle is equal to the radius of the circle.

9. The appellant may or may not be the one who "lost" in the lower court, since the "winning" party may have appealed only one particular aspect of the case such as the amount of damages.

10. The burden of care is frequently on women wives—and daughters—who are themselves aging.

11. The first step in proper viewing of a model is to identify the two crucial components of the center of interest (the piece of the image at which the viewer is looking and the viewer's position) in relation to the model.

12. A building containing a large proportion of steel or a room with line-of-sight obstacles or radio-wave absorbing materials (such as cardboard or heavy fabric) near an access point will likely cause disruption to wireless transmissions.

13. States operating under determinate sentencing guidelines often require that inmates serve a short period of time (such as 90 days) in reentry parole, a form of mandatory release.

14. The three kinds of film (periapical, bitewing, and occlusal) are manufactured in sizes 0-4.

15. A powerline capacitor (also called a stiffening capacitor) refers to a large capacitor of 0.25 farad or larger.

16. Biopsies (to determine benign or malignant lesions) are performed by surgically removing a small specimen of the abnormal tissue for further diagnosis.

17. Jailed women (12% of the country's jail population) face a number of special problems.

18. In traditional forward auctioning (sometimes called a Yankee auction) shoppers make offers for a desired item.

19. You can save any view displayed in a viewport—once saved it is easily restored.

20. Cyanosis (a bluish tinge) is most evident in the nail beds, lips, and buccal mucosa.

21. References to any appellate court decisions will usually include a series of numbers and abbreviations known collectively as a citation.

22. Wrong values in a circuit (such as an incorrect resistor value) can cause improper operation.

23. In the electrical utilities field, kilowatts (kW) and megawatts (MW) are common units.

24. The ethical guidelines governing the paralegal come from a variety of potential sources (codes of ethics, statutes, and case law).

25. Boil water—this is the most practical and inexpensive method to sterilize the home.

UNDERLINING AND *ITALICS*

EXERCISE 6.4:

1. The Basics of Paralegal Studies by David Goodrich is the beginning text for paralegal studies.

2. For electronics, we use Electronic Fundamentals by Thomas Floyd.

3. Piaget's Origin of Intelligence in Children is a landmark text for understanding the different levels at which human beings progress.

4. AutoCAD in 3 Dimensions: Using AutoCAD 2004 was written to provide the information students need to compete in the job market.

5. The Home Depot has been voted America's Most Admired Retailer by Fortune magazine for many consecutive years.

6. According to Prisoners in 2000, the number of women incarcerated for drug crimes has risen 108% since 1990.

7. Information about dental assisting can be found in Richardson and Barton's The Dental Assistant.

8. Automotive Technology: Principles, Diagnosis, and Service by James Halderman and Chase Mitchell is organized around the eight automobile test areas.

9. The engine of the president's plane, Air Force I, is vastly different than that of an automobile engine.

10. The Running Man, a film with Dustin Hoffman, shows tooth extraction without lidocaine.

11. As written in "On-the-Job Stress in Policing" in the National Institute of Justice Journal (January 2000), stress is a natural component of police work.

12. With MIS Cases: Decision Making with Application Software by M. Lisa Miller, students will prepare to make management level decisions with the most complete and interactive management information systems casebook on the market.

13. AutoCAD resources can be found on www.autocad.com.

14. Peck's Psychological Aspects of Aging reveals psychological developments in the second half of life.

15. In 1975, the first personal computer was introduced by Altair, and Popular Science magazine featured it on the cover of the January 1975 issue.

16. Certified legal assistant information can be found by going to www.nala.org.

17. The electronics manual, <u>Power On!</u>, is a primary source of basic circuitry information.

18. Discussions of severe skin diseases can be found in <u>Dermatology Nursing</u> by R. Jackson.

19. The article, "Designing Your House," appears in <u>AutoCAD Design for Today</u>.

20. Losses from fraudulent and misleading business transactions conducted over the Internet are expected to reach $15 billion annually by 2005 according to a recent report in <u>CIO Magazine</u>.

21. "What Say Should Victims Have?" in <u>Time</u> magazine addresses victims' rights in the United States.

22. When I'm in the dentist's waiting room, I read the <u>Dental Practice Management Encyclopedia</u>.

23. A significant Internet resource for automotive technology is <u>www.cars.net</u>.

24. <u>NYPD Blue</u> is an accurate depiction of crime in New York.

25. Features titled <u>Information Technology in Practice</u> relate examples of successful IT use.

QUOTATION MARKS

EXERCISE 6.5:

1. The "just deserts" model of criminal sentencing insists that punishment should be the central theme of the justice process.

2. The dentist told the patient that wearing braces would be necessary to correct the gap between the front teeth.

3. "My car," said the woman, "is making noises like a washing machine."

4. The jury foreman told the judge that the defendant was guilty and should be put in jail for a hundred years.

5. My "fail-safe" computer system includes duplicate components; should one system malfunction, the other will take over to keep the computer running.

6. Mrs. Walters told the designer, "Please include a pool room in my house. My husband," she said, "loves to play pool."

7. Feeling faint, the patient wobbled into the emergency room and whispered, "Help me!"

8. "Paying Your Electric Bill" which appeared in the <u>Washington Post</u>, helped me to understand the rising cost of electricity.

9. "Procedural rules differ from one state to another," said the paralegal.

10. In his opening statement, the attorney told the jury that the defendant is "non compos mentis."

11. The teacher asked if anyone had a question. "Please explain bipolar voltage dividers to me," said the student.

12. The apothecary uses units of weight called the "scruple," "the dram," "the ounce," and the "pound."

13. In explaining parametric types, the teacher said, "The parameters of a type 3ES parametric symbol allow it to be scaled uniformly in all three axes."

14. During the early days of information technology, the coming of the "paperless office" was proclaimed.

15. The Juvenile Justice Bulletin says that "Children who remain at large for a few weeks will resort to theft or prostitution as a method of self support."

16. "NO," screamed the dental technician as the door opened. "I'm developing X-Rays."

17. "You're going to charge me WHAT?" said the customer to the car repair technician.

18. "When diagnosing any brake problem," claimed the boss, "apply the parking brake and count the clicks."

19. Have you ever read the poem "Ode to the Orthodontist"?

20. "She killed him in self-defense," said the attorney in his opening statement to the jury.

21. Backup procedures, also called "backup copies," describe how and when to make extra copies.

22. The show, Home Improvement, is a long way from AutoCAD drafting.

23. I just love the song "Doctor Cure All My Ills."

24. In explaining diodes, the electrician said that a diode is a semiconductive device made with a single pn junction.

25. The attorney told the paralegal, "Some of your responsibilities will include interviewing clients, preparing court pleadings, and investigations."

EXERCISE 6.6:

A. Now that you've made the choice to enroll in college, you've added new responsibilities to your life: attending classes and studying, to mention a couple. Your time is now even more limited. Most likely, you will find it difficult to do all that you used to without the help of those around you: your employer, family members, friends, teachers, college peers, and the college administrative staff. Many adult college freshmen already have a strong network of family and friends. Even if you live alone, you can develop a strong support network through friends, co-workers, and fellow students. But to get help, you must ask for it. Make the choice to ask for help from all those who can give it to you.

B. Stress and pressure—two forces that most people deal with every day of their lives. As adults, you're already familiar with the feelings that stress can produce. You're aware of what it means to cope with everyday pressures—working, paying bills, meeting the needs of your family and friends, making time for yourself, and completing countless other tasks and obligations. Now, as an adult college student you may be wondering how you will be able to cope with adding the additional responsibilities of school (studying, attending classes, tests) to your already full plate. You may be asking yourself how you will meet and deal with the many challenges that college will present. While stress and pressure are natural parts of life, you can learn to deal with these forces in productive ways: you can make choices that will improve your physical health, increase your energy, and improve your attitude to help you through the collegiate process and to promote a better chance of success.

C. Tests are not arbitrary lists of questions devised by instructors. They are, in fact, well organized, structured, and commonly formatted questions designed and developed to measure a student's knowledge of a subject. Tests come in a variety of forms—true/false, multiple choice, short answer, fill in, and essay—and each of these forms follows a predictable structure. Recognizing and knowing these structures can aid in your ability to answer questions correctly and appropriately, thus achieving a better grade. In addition, understanding the test format can reduce stress; you'll know what to expect and how a particular type of test "works." Learning and comprehending the format and nature of different kinds of tests will make you more confident in your responses.

D. Maximizing the classroom experience means being prepared for class, participating actively in class, and taking good class notes, among other things. But what if you're struggling with trying to take notes or what if you miss a class or two or what if personal issues distract you from paying attention in class? Maximizing the classroom experience also means getting all that you can out of class and if, for whatever reason, you're unable to, **get help!** If you're struggling with class, ask teachers for direction, tutors for assistance, or fellow classmates for class notes. A successful classroom experience relies on your ability to understand the material, be prepared for class, get the assignments, and do the work—if you're unable to, get the help you need.

E. Students who are not experienced in writing sometimes have misconceptions about the writing process. They project certain ideas about writing papers that cloud their thinking and automatically establish obstacles to creativity and the writing process. Perhaps because they were poor writers in high school, some students believe that the college experience will be the same. If previous teachers criticized papers and ideas, then current college teachers will be just as critical. Maybe some students tell themselves, "I can't write—never could and never will." Some college students tell themselves repeatedly they don't know how to write and cannot learn, so why would they even want to try? Maybe students believe that writing is "no big deal." It's easy enough to do it the night before the paper is due—spend a couple of hours at the computer. Or, maybe students believe that higher intelligence equals a better paper; if I'm smart, then I'll get a better grade. If I'm not smart, why would I want to put anything in writing in the first place? And finally, perhaps some students think that they will not ever have the need to write in their particular careers, so why should they need to learn at all? It is just these misconceptions about writing that prohibit you from writing. It is just these false ideas about writing that inhibit your spontaneous abilities. It is just these judgments about writing that halt your natural creativity. And it is just these obstacles that prevent you from learning the skills you need to advance your career. Now that you're in college, you may want to reconsider your perceptions about written expression.

Part IV: Grammar
Chapter 7: Agreement, Voice, and Qualifiers
SUBJECT/VERB AGREEMENT

EXERCISE 7.1:

1. **Immobility** refer/<u>refers</u> to a reduction in the amount and control of movement a person has.

2. The most unique **feature** of the AIT format <u>is</u>/are the innovative emory-in-cassette drive interface system.

3. **Criteria** for a properly placed wedge require/<u>requires</u> that the wedge ensure stability of the matrix band.

4. The **internal windings** <u>contain</u>/contains approximately the same number of turns but are made from different gauge wire.

5. After the important **distinction** between primary and secondary authority <u>is</u>/are drawn, both state and federal material will be analyzed.

6. The **Thevenin equivalent form** of any two-terminal resistive circuit consist/<u>consists</u> of an equivalent voltage source and an equivalent resistance.

7. **Every one** of the areas in the blue cross-hatching represent/<u>represents</u> the effective plotting area.

8. **Constitutive criminology** refer/<u>refers</u> to the process by which human beings create an ideology of crime that sustain/<u>sustains</u> it as a concrete reality.

9. The **Midtown Community Court** in New York City show/<u>shows</u> how community courts work.

10. This **list** of radio buttons allow/<u>allows</u> you to tell AutoCAD what parts of your drawing you want to plot.

11. The **sum** of all the voltage drops around a single closed path in a circle <u>is</u>/are equal to the total source voltage in that closed path.

12. **Either** the attorney or the paralegal consult/<u>consults</u> with the plaintiff.

13. A thorough **inspection** of the spark plugs lead/<u>leads</u> to the root cause of an engine performance problem.

14. The main **component** of composite restorative materials <u>is</u>/are polymethyl methacrylate, hydrogen peroxide, calcium hydroxide, or inorganic filler.

15. The **choice** of cables affect/<u>affects</u> the network card.

16. A **vesicle** or **blister** cause/<u>causes</u> an erosion and illustrate/<u>illustrates</u> secondary lesions.

17. **Each** of the organisms cause/<u>causes</u> infection.

18. **All** the processing capabilities of the control unit and ALU <u>reside</u>/resides on a single computer chip.

19. **Formation** of tooth buds lead/<u>leads</u> to development of primary and succedaneous teeth.

20. Temperature or pressure **controls** <u>prevent</u>/prevents the freezing of the evaporator.

21. The **group** of nine justices <u>is</u>/are the highest court in the country.

22. The physical **arrangement** of components on a PC board bear/<u>bears</u> no resemblance to the actual electrical relationships.

23. The **results** of the rotation is/<u>are</u> dramatically affected by your choice of base point.

24. The **number** of new and innovative defenses being tried on juries and judges today <u>is</u>/are staggering.

25. In the *Miranda* decision, the **Supreme Court** require/<u>requires</u> that **officers** <u>provide</u>/provides warnings to potential criminals.

ACTIVE/PASSIVE VOICE

EXERCISE 7.2:

1. Civil law contains rules for contracts.

2. Creating polar rays requires some explanation.

3. Figure 7-16 shows the basic structure of a solenoid.

4. Researches do not quote directly from encyclopedias in appellate briefs or memoranda of law.

5. After the engine is rebuilt, replacing the oil pump ensures positive lubrication and long pump life.

6. The flowmeter controls the volume of gas administration to the patient.

7. The control unit does not execute instructions.

8. The client record should describe the client's ongoing status.

9. Cartridges are the most commonly used form of tape storage today.

10. Psychologic homeostasis refers to the emotional or psychological balance or a state of mental well-being.

11. An assessment of the lungs and thorax—inspection, palpation, percussion, and auscultation—includes all methods of examination.

12. ISPs typically charge a monthly service fee.

13. Endocrine glands produce chemical mediators called hormones.

14. Kirchhoff states that the voltage will drop in proportion to the resistance.

15. The courts handle a wide variety of cases.

16. Electrolytic capacitors offer higher capacitance values than mica or ceramic capacitors.

17. AutoCAD printing and plotting requires an understanding of the relationships among model space, paper space, plot styles, page setups, and layouts.

18. Based on their judgment and assessment, parole boards grant paroles.

19. Prisonization refers to the learning of convict values, attitudes, roles, and even language.

20. AutoCAD provides two commands for entering text in a drawing.

21. Figure 5-21 shows a general case of *n* resistors in parallel.

22. Society as a whole punishes those who engage in certain kinds of behavior that unreasonably interfere with the rights of others.

23. The piston ring transfers to the channeling rod the force produced by combustion chamber pressures and piston inertia.

24. The modified Stillman technique incorporates a rolling stroke and a vibratory stroke.

25. Microcomputers contain specific microprocessor chips as their CPU.

MISPLACED AND DANGLING MODIFIERS

EXERCISE 7.3:

1. In the early days, grand juries served a far different purpose.

2. The stretches require careful selection of multiple grips, just like the ones you have performed.

3. When a resistor is used in a circuit, its power rating should be greater than the maximum power that it will have to handle. **OK**

4. That index, which may be several volumes in length, is organized alphabetically.

5. Fuel injectors are usually controlled by varying the pulse width. **OK**

6. Always wash your hands with antimicrobial soap before and after you remove gloves.

7. Most PCs manufactured today, including laptop computers, have at least two USB ports built in.

8. Generally, this technique is not used to percuss the thorax, but is useful in percussing an adult's sinuses.

9. If the patient complains of numbness, peculiar sensations, or paralysis, the practitioner should check sensation more carefully over flexor and extensor surfaces on the limbs of the patient.

10. Inserting or removing memory, chips, or boards, as well as storage or peripheral devices, changes the configuration of a computer.

11. A nurse should always assess a client's health status and obtain a medication history prior to giving any new medication.

12. Over the last few decades, robots have moved from the realm of science fiction to the factory floor.

13. Always clean tissue side of tray and disinfect before seating in the patient's mouth.

14. If the engine does not feel or smell hot, it is possible that the problem is a faulty hot light sensor or gauge.

15. While the text addresses the traditional ways in which legal research is conducted, it is important to understand that there are now additional options available to the researcher as a result of widespread use of computers.

16. For the amplifier to operate properly, certain bias voltages must remain constant and, therefore, remove only AC voltages.

17. The CHAMFER command sequence is almost identical to the FILLET command.

18. The direct examiner may again question the witness at the conclusion.

19. All these boxes have a very similar format.

20. All the ground points in a circuit are electrically the same and are therefore common points.

21. When the decisions are rendered by a group of judges, all the judges may not agree with the conclusions or reasoning of the one writing for the majority.

22. A technician's hands always should be washed thoroughly after touching used engine oils, transmission fluids, and greases.

23. The shade of one's teeth may be affected by either extrinsic or intrinsic stains; tooth bleaching is implemented primarily for aesthetics.

24. All systems have a practical limit to the number of ports that can be added.

25. While the patient exhales, exert a gradual and gentle downward and forward pressure beneath the costal.

Chapter 8: Sentence Errors

FRAGMENTS

EXERCISE 8.1: Responses will vary; however, all should include subject and verb.

1. From the back of the operating room, I could hear the scream of the newborn as it was birthed.

2. The broken chair was moved from the dentist's office to the shop for repairs.

3. Visiting the dentist twice a year for a check up and cleaning is essential for maintaining the health of your teeth and gums.

4. When checking a patient's heartbeat, a stethoscope is used.

5. Screeching to a halt, the ambulance stopped to avoid hitting the pedestrian.

6. Our apologies, your appointment, for now, is delayed an hour.

7. Use a syringe to administer the shot.

8. We wear only clean, blue scrubs and masks in our operating rooms.

9. He concentrated on passing the forceps to the obstetrician.

10. Pharmacy technicians, surgical technicians, and medical assistants study their disciplines for two years before they are able to work in the field.

11. Before selling his work, the architect must know the value of reviewing drawings and designs.

12. The producer requested that Steve animate the scene with all of the characters in the story.

13. Designing a new room is quite a challenge since the dimensions of the space contradict the owner's needs.

14. His proposal included everything that is necessary for building his dream home, including plans for the garden.

15. Using 3D imagery allows the mechanical engineer to display his design from different angles.

16. Locating the tire jack in a packed trunk can take much time.

17. While driving through the neighborhood, he noticed that the engine was smoking.

18. This year's two-door sedan has more room than last year's model.

19. He worked as quickly as he could though there were cars waiting in line.

20. There are problems with the drive shaft to be fixed.

21. Many of our jails, full with drug-addicted criminals, need more funds for rehabilitation programs.

22. Handcuffs, bulletproof vest, gun, and mace are required for your belt.

23. His sentencing hearing is scheduled to begin in the morning.

24. She noticed the car burglar as she patrolled the shopping mall neighborhood.

25. The judge stated that she believes in justice, swift and fair for all.

26. He decided that he wanted to study criminal justice while watching the crime scene show on television.

27. The officers loved to patrol where the children play.

28. The paper reported that felonies are on the increase since the beginning of the year.

29. Did you attend the career fair held last month?

30. He advised that I practice before interviewing for the position.

31. While connecting the wiring for the fan, he discovered a beehive in the ceiling.

32. It is important to consider many factors when choosing the proper circuit board.

33. Avoiding water when blow-drying your hair is one of the safety tips listed.

34. Be sure to ground the wires before working with the circuits.

35. Knowing about voltmeters will reduce the work required for installation.

36. Defending the plaintiff will not be an easy task because of his past media exposure.

37. In preparation for jury selection tomorrow, the attorney met with a psychologist to form specific questions.

38. We have completed 32 real estate closings for the month.

39. When the court opens in the morning, I plan to file an injunction against the company.

40. He has three subpoenas to be served by tomorrow at 5:00 P.M.

41. She is in search of a job that provides a weekly salary and benefits.

42. Wade decided that he is ready for a career change, one that will allow him to achieve his goal of helping others.

43. With the job completed, he is filled with pride by the result.

44. Searching the unemployment advertisements is not the only effective tool for looking for a new job.

45. Margaret hit a car as she was rushing to work yesterday.

46. Once they have graduated from college, many people prefer to work in a field that relates to their degree.

47. Since I will be graduating from college this month, I have planned to take a vacation.

48. While completing my homework, I had to remember the lesson from last week.

49. Partially completed, the work was not ready to be reviewed by the supervisor.

50. I have not worked eight-hour days for weeks.

RUN-ONS

EXERCISE 8.2:

1. The medical assistant left for work early in the morning. She stopped for coffee at the coffee shop before driving to the office.

2. Working for others has always been difficult for her, so she has decided to be a contractor. This allows her to create her own schedule and to charge more money hourly.

3. Her cell phone rang many times before she was able to finish cleaning the patient's teeth. So, she allowed it to ring even though it disturbed the dentist who was working next door.

4. Often, the doctor asked for assistance when administering shots. He needs new glasses and so, cannot see the veins as well as before.

5. The other night, Noah received a call from the night supervisor asking him to substitute for another technician. Even though he had already worked the two shifts prior, he agreed.

6. Before the ambulance could take the patient to the emergency room, the driver had to change the flat tire. It was caused by a nail that the vehicle ran over.

7. The patient called his dentist's office for an emergency appointment because he had an abscess. It caused him tremendous pain and made him feel sick even though he realized its existence a week ago.

8. After witnessing the fall, Georgia called the doctor to the hallway to help the patient who had passed out. The patient had not eaten before taking her medication earlier that morning.

9. Where are the sutures? Where are the forceps? Do you know where the extra packages of gauze are?

10. Now that I have completed my clinical rounds, I am eager to begin my search for a new job. I know that it will not be easy to find a job in this area of the country.

11. Does anyone know when the updated drawing program will be available for us to test? We are working on a design that needs the new multi-creation feature so that we can show the client a variety of dimensions.

12. While mapping the schematics for the power grid, the engineer discovered a design flaw. This was created during the revision meeting with the clients that continued for hours, though everyone was tired.

13. Where are the plans for the outdoor deck? Did you misplace them or are they, perhaps, in your car? We need them for this meeting.

14. He reported that his truck broke down somewhere between two highway exits for the next town north. Though he is uncertain as to the cause, he knows that the starter needs replacing.

15. Oil changes are not difficult to complete unless you do not have the proper tools. Then, it is impossible to do it properly; in fact, you could damage your engine.

16. Last night, there was a violent windstorm in the mid-west. The destruction was so fierce that it levied damage upon town after town, leaving thousands without power.

17. Jayne called an electrician to install a ceiling fan and to install an additional electrical outlet in her house. He cannot come for another week, which is problematic.

18. Late to her advanced circuitry class, Sheila worried that she missed the review for the test. The test will be given next Wednesday night and next Thursday night.

19. Although there are better ways to connect the wires for the stereo, the technician insisted on using the factory speaker cables that were packaged with the system. He wanted to keep the cost of the job to less than one hundred dollars.

20. The five steps in Thevenin's Theorem provide that an equivalent circuit can be used to replace the original circuit. This can be done even if the circuits are slightly different from each other.

21. We advised that the client purchase three laptops, two desktop computers, a server and five printers. All of these will be networked together to create an office that allows staff members to work on projects separately in their own offices.

22. Sometime between last night at 6:00 P.M. and this morning 5:00 A.M., a virus attacked our operating system. When I arrived in the office at 6:00 A.M., I noticed that the screen, which should have displayed my screensaver, was blank.

23. Excited about the release of the new beta software for the word processing program, the team anxiously completed the last data tests. These are required before marketing it to the public.

24. Please schedule an appointment with Mr. Mercado tomorrow since he has complained that his printer is not working properly. Be sure to take an extra ink cartridge with you because, I think that the problem is that the other one is empty.

25. Has anyone seen the latest posting on the webpage? I heard that our company is featured as one of the hottest design firms in town. If that is true, we can create a link from our site to that one.

26. I am frustrated because I have tried to upload my assignment for the past three hours. I continue to receive the message that the server is busy or broken. So, the assignment partially loads and then seems to be stuck.

27. Someone told me that I should schedule an appointment with a legal assistant to discuss my options for filing divorce. If I do not do this, I might not be able to keep most of my property.

28. When we decided to purchase our home, we hired an attorney to review the closing documents because we had never bought a home before. We wanted to be sure that we understood all of the language in the contract.

29. The legal assistant spent most of the night conducting research for the trial scheduled for the following day. The attorney that he worked for had discovered some new information that might be relevant.

30. I heard that Ms. Lowry's torte class is very difficult and that she assigns a lot of homework and gives many tests. She believes that this helps students to learn the information.

31. To find a job in my field, I need to use the Internet to research information about salary, location, and anything else that will help me to choose the best option. One option, that suits my values and my lifestyle preferences, is to earn more money.

32. Before graduation, I am going to write cover letters and a resume so that I will be ready to search for a job and work in my field. I want to use my skills to help people who are working with the criminal justice system.

33. My study skills have improved since enrolling in college classes because I have had to learn to write papers, organize my activities into a schedule, and conduct research. I know that these skills will help me to succeed in my career once I complete my degree requirements.

34. Learning to write clearly, using proper grammar and punctuation, can take time and practice. This is necessary, I know, so that I will be able to write competently once I am working in my career.

35. Many times I have considered withdrawing from my college classes because I felt overwhelmed by the work. I have also felt the pressure of completing assignments by the deadlines and worrying about my grades. But somehow, I manage to complete everything and then feel better.

Chapter 9: Sentence Connectors

COORDINATING CONJUNCTIONS

EXERCISE 9.1:

1. Written law is of two types: substantive <u>and</u> procedural.

2. The right button on your mouse can also be used in place of the Enter key sometimes, <u>but</u> in most cases, there will be an intervening step involving a shortcut menu with choices.

3. The curve showing how these two quantities (*B <u>and</u> H*) are related is called the *B-H* curve, <u>or</u> the hysteresis curve.

4. Problems in reducing an issue to written form may be an indication that the researcher has not <u>yet</u> clearly formulated the issue.

5. The belt is generally considered to be quieter, <u>but</u> it requires periodic replacement.

6. Fluoride toxicity is a potential danger if the correct dosage of fluoride is not administered, <u>so</u> be very careful.

7. Streaming also makes it possible for many users to retrieve the same file of audio, video, <u>or</u> other information simultaneously.

8. Characteristics of pit <u>and</u> fissure sealants include self-cured <u>or</u> light-cured polymerization <u>and</u> acid etching.

9. <u>Neither</u> engine oil <u>nor</u> break fluid should be applied to a Teflon oil seal.

10. Many, <u>but</u> not all, of the states have separate state reporters, <u>and</u> citations of cases in such states should contain references to both the state <u>and</u> regional reporters.

11. This particular instrument can be used to measure <u>either</u> direct current <u>or</u> alternating current quantities.

12. You can select individual entities on the screen by pointing to them one by one, <u>yet</u> in complex drawings this is often inefficient.

13. Criminal trials under our system of justice are built around the adversarial system <u>and</u> that central to this system is the advocacy model.

14. Private attorneys <u>either</u> have their own legal practices <u>or</u> work for law firms in which they are partners <u>or</u> employees.

15. To define movement with a vector, all AutoCAD needs is a distance <u>and</u> a direction.

EXERCISE 9.2:

1. The LCD requires little current, <u>but</u> it is difficult to see in low light and is slow to respond.

2. Any item, including custom trays <u>and</u> dental waxes, that has been used in the mouth carries the potential for cross contamination, <u>so</u> always disinfect or dispose of used materials.

3. You can also provide your own text, <u>but</u> that would defeat the purpose of setting up a coordinate system that automatically gives you the distances from the intersection of the two lines.

4. A person cannot be tried, sentenced, <u>or</u> punished while insane.

5. The appellees contend that there are literally hundreds of other pieces of property of the same size <u>and</u> shape within the very same development <u>and</u> that the appellant therefore cannot establish the requisite uniqueness of the property, <u>yet</u> this argument overlooks one very important factor.

6. Either the deglazing hone <u>or</u> the sizing hone is used for cylinder service.

7. Neither a desktop <u>nor</u> laptop computer can ever replace the human brain.

8. Often, a section of the electronic component may be damaged, <u>yet</u> will not fail until several days or weeks later.

9. On the basis of the judge's finding, the person is arrested <u>and</u> taken to a magistrate's hearing <u>and</u> notified of the pending charges, the right to counsel, <u>and</u> any potential adjustment of the amount set for bail, <u>so</u> there is no need for a preliminary hearing because the judge has already determined that probable cause exists.

10. The types of teeth are the incisors, canines, premolars, <u>and</u> molars.

11. Line operations are field <u>or</u> supervisory activities, <u>but</u> staff operations include support roles, like administration.

12. Remember, the procedure listed is a general list of how to enter <u>and</u> use the LINE command, <u>so</u> it is for reference and clarity only.

13. Air-core <u>and</u> ferrite-core transformers generally are used for high-frequency applications <u>and</u> consist of windings in an insulating shell that is hollow <u>or</u> constructed of the ferrite.

14. Neither cybercrime <u>nor</u> information-technology crime was ever conceived of in the 1900s.

15. Supragingival calculus occurs above the gum line, <u>and</u> subgingival occurs below the gum line.

SUBORDINATING CONJUNCTIONS

EXERCISE 9.4:

1. <u>Before</u> creating the plot area window, look at the Plot Scale panel on the right of the dialog box.

2. <u>As</u> you learned in this chapter, capacitors are used in certain types of amplifiers for coupling AC signals and blocking DC voltages.

3. <u>If</u> the defendant is found guilty, the defense attorney will be involved in arguments at sentencing.

4. The server may be required by state law to sign a document <u>after</u> the service of process has been affected.

5. <u>Because</u> of regulations, containers used to transport regulated waste must be identified with a red biohazard label.

6. Hypothermia may result <u>when</u> the body is exposed to severely cold temperatures.

7. <u>During</u> assembly of system boards, the leads of the microprocessor package are inserted into holes in the circuit board.

8. <u>When</u> the ignition switch is turned to the start position, the motion of the plunger into the solenoid causes the starter drive to move.

9. You can find any topic of interest on the computer <u>since</u> so many databases are now available.

10. <u>Even though</u> people who have narcolepsy sleep very well at night, they nod off several times a day.

11. Protective, visible light eyewear is required to protect the eyes from retinal damage <u>because</u> of the potential for physical harm.

12. <u>Whenever</u> the Constitution is subjected to interpretation by the Courts, the resulting court precedent may have the effect of "amending" the Constitution.

13. Changing fonts is a simple matter <u>because</u> there is much room for confusion in the use of the words style and font.

14. <u>After</u> the *Miranda* decision was handed down, some hailed it as ensuring the protection of individual rights under the Constitution.

15. <u>Since</u> each resistor has the same current through it, the voltage drops are proportional to the resistance values.

EXERCISE 9.5:

1. <u>If</u> the defendant is a first time felon, the judge may give him a lighter sentence.

2. <u>When</u> you save a drawing file, AutoCAD allows you to save different versions of the same drawing under different names.

3. One can be sued for breach of a contract <u>whether</u> it is oral or written.

4. <u>Before</u> you touch the patient's mouth, be certain you are wearing gloves.

5. Clearly state the priorities of care and care that is due <u>after</u> the shift begins.

6. Acceptance and processing of orders submitted by customers are <u>among</u> the most common activities of business.

7. <u>Because</u> the air density is lower at high altitudes, the power that a normal engine can develop is greatly reduced.

8. Laptop computers can save battery power <u>while</u> the computer is in hibernation mode.

9. <u>Although</u> efforts have been made to control the costs of health care, these costs continue to increase.

10. An action may or may not be regarded as a decision on the merits <u>when</u> it is dismissed.

11. <u>Unless</u> the patient carries dental insurance, payment should be collected at each visit.

12. <u>Before</u> your array definition is complete, AutoCAD needs to know how far apart to place all these circles.

13. Vehicles present a special law enforcement problem <u>because</u> they are highly mobile.

14. <u>Since</u> voltages must be measured at several points in a circuit, the ground lead can be clipped to ground at one point in the circuit and left there.

15. A sophisticated approach to biological theorizing about crime causation has arisen <u>over</u> the past few decades.

EXERCISE 9.7:

1. researching law, drafting documents, **interviewing witnesses**, organizing evidence

2. press, indicate, **answer**, move

3. feelings about self, reactions from others, one's perceptions of these reactions, attitudes, values, many of life's experiences **OK**

4. troubleshoot series-parallel circuits, determine the effects in a short circuit, **locate opens and shorts**

5. incisors used for biting, canines used for tearing, **premolars and molars used for crushing and grinding**

6. reliable, economical, compact, **convenient**

7. victims experience uncertainties, traumas, and **fears**

8. intake or exhaust valve, piston rings, cylinder head gasket **OK**

9. enforcing the law, apprehending offenders, **preventing crime**, preserving the peace, **providing services**

10. to manage detail, to give a common meaning, to document features, **to locate errors**

11. proteins, carbohydrates, fats, minerals, vitamins, water **OK**

12. define resistance and discuss its characteristics, name and define the unit of resistance, **describe the basic types of resistance**, determine resistance value

13. **quieting the mind**, focusing on the present, releasing anxieties about the future

14. beginning a new drawing, **drawing a vertical line**, typing the line

15. deliberation, premeditation, solicitation **OK**

EXERCISE 9.8:

1. Prior to trial, the paralegal may be called upon to locate and contact all witnesses, to organize court pleadings, and to accompany the attorney to trial.

2. The procedure for entering multiline text using MTEXT includes typing *t*, specifying the first corner, typing the text, and clicking OK.

3. Explain to the patient what you are going to do, why it is necessary, and how to cooperate.

4. In a case of a short in the circuit, you may find a faulty wire clipping, a solder splash, or a bad touching leads to the problem.

5. The bone that supports the teeth is called the alveolar bone or the cancellous bone or the medullary bone.

6. The participants may be in the same room, or linked up by a local area network, or geographically dispersed and interconnected over a wide area network.

7. The type of intermediate sentencing the judge imposes is based on whether the offender committed the crime for money, for the excitement it afforded, for revenge, or for "the thrill of it."

8. To perform an accurate compression test, remove all spark plugs, open the block throttle and the choke, and thread a compression gauge into one spark plug and crank the engine.

9. Laws serve a variety of purposes including preventing the victimization of innocents, sustainng existing power relationships, upholding established patterns of social privilege, and maintaining values.

10. Information technology professionals are responsible for developing, maintaining, or operating the hardware and software associated with computers and communications networks.

11. Sodium fluoride 2% offers many advantages: it does not stain teeth; it remains a stable solution when stored in a polyethylene bottle; it has a less objectionable taste; gingival irritation does not occur.

12. Capacitor values are indicated on the body of the capacitor by numerical labels or phanumerical labels or color codes.

13. Normally, older clients have unaltered perception of light touch and superficial pain, a decreased perception of deep pain, and a decreased perception of temperature stimuli.

14. The SPLINEDIT command gives you additional options, including the option to change the tolerance, to add fit points for greater definition, or to delete unnecessary points.

15. It is unethical for paralegals to enter into partnerships, associations, or corporations with attorneys in a business involving the practice of law.

16. Dimensions can be edited in many of the same ways other objects are edited; they can be moved, copied, stretched, rotated, trimmed, or extended.

17. The infection control nurse records and analyzes statistics, educates, and implements the mandated OSHA plan.

18. Troubleshooting involves applying logical thinking, having a thorough knowledge of circuits, and forming a logical plan of attack.

19. The substance within the bone, known as bone marrow, produces red blood cells, platelets, and white blood cells.

20. The basic purposes of policing in democratic societies are enforcing and supporting the laws of society, investigating crimes and apprehending offenders, preventing crime, ensuring domestic peace and tranquility, and providing the community with needed enforcement-related services.

Chapter 10: Pronoun Usage

PRONOUN AGREEMENT

EXERCISE 10.1:

      A   *P*   *P*

1. *George spent last night completing his writing assignment for his case law class.*

      A1   *A2*   *P2 P1*

2. To date, <u>Charlie</u> has not encountered a <u>problem</u> like <u>this</u>; <u>he</u> is uncertain of how to fix the programming error.

      A   *P*

3. <u>Interviewing</u> is not an easy process because <u>it</u> challenges people to use quick thinking.

      A   *A*   *A*   *P*

4. <u>Mario</u>, <u>Shawntee</u>, and <u>Jack</u> are going to the conference to demonstrate <u>their</u> robotic arm model.

      A   *P*

5. The <u>driver</u> watches the road signs carefully so that <u>he</u> will not miss the turn.

      A   *P*

6. Whenever <u>Steve</u> discussed the movie project, <u>he</u> argued about whether the animation should be in 2D or 3D.

      A   *P*

7. The schedule indicates that <u>May</u> is enrolled in the four classes that <u>she</u> needs for graduation.

          A   *P*

8. Remember to wear your <u>scrubs</u> for class on Monday, because you will need <u>them</u> when you go to the hospital to watch an operation.

          A   *P*

9. Torte <u>law</u> is not a difficult subject to study, though <u>it</u> can be if you do not complete your readings before class.

          A1   *A2*   *P1*

10. It is <u>somebody</u> else's <u>job</u> to complete the paperwork though <u>he/she</u> may not be aware

      P2

of <u>that</u>.

                                      P   *A*

11. Worried about the trojan virus on <u>his</u> computer, <u>Vinnie</u> called the company's computer technician for assistance.

       A   *P*   *P*

12. <u>Juana</u> learned that <u>she</u> is to be promoted next week because of <u>her</u> excellent work as a probation officer.

          A   *P*

13. The <u>electrician</u>, puzzled because <u>he</u> could not find the short in the circuit, decided to test all of the circuits.

              A   *P*

14. Patricia started the <u>car</u> this morning to find that <u>it</u> blows smoke from the tailpipe.

          A1   *P1*

15. Today, <u>James</u> is being released from the detention center, <u>he</u> wants to thank his counselor,

      A2   *P1*

<u>Pedro</u> for helping <u>him</u>.

      A1   *A2*   *P1*   *P2*

16. <u>Frank</u> created the <u>designs</u> for the house; <u>he</u> is proud of <u>them</u>.

                                        A   *P*

17. During the violent windstorm, some electrical <u>poles</u> fell as <u>they</u> had been loosened by past storms.

                                A   *P*

18. Please, ask someone to review your <u>resume</u> before sending <u>it</u> to companies.

19. Hard work and perseverance helped <u>Jim</u> to excel in his studies; <u>he</u> will continue to work like this on his job.

20. <u>Keisha</u> cannot decide whether <u>she</u> should work in a hospital or in a doctor's office.

EXERCISE 10.2:

1. he

2. they

3. her

4. he/she

5. he/she

6. they

7. We

8. us

9. them

10. it

11. they

12. it

13. he/she

14. you

15. he/she

EXERCISE 10.3:

1. Our last surgical procedures class ended last Tuesday. <u>We</u> are excited about the prospect of working in a hospital in the operating room. There are so many operations that <u>we</u> did not have the opportunity to assist with during <u>our</u> internships. Personally, I am eager to use <u>my</u> new skills to assist surgeons.

2. The patient needs to lie in the prone position on the table. <u>He/she</u> will then be asked to lie still as the nurse takes <u>his/her</u> blood pressure and vital signs. <u>It</u> will take only a few minutes to complete the procedure. We will then meet in the lab to view <u>his/her</u> x-rays that were taken last week; <u>this</u> should help <u>us</u> to make a diagnosis.

3. We learned in our career skills class that in order for us to be offered the jobs that we want, we have to write clear resumes. Writing them was difficult for us since we had not written resumes before. Resumes, in order to be effective, must contain our education and work experience. I was pleased with mine when I finished.

4. While driving home from the market, one of my tires drove over a nail. Now, it was flat and I had to change it before I could return home with the groceries. Not remembering how to change a flat tire, I called my mechanic for assistance. He/she told me to use my car jack to raise the car. Next, I used a wrench to loosen the lug nuts; one of them took a long time to remove. Tired from the effort, I rested against the car, it was still warm. It was then that I remembered that the food was still in the car. I was worried that the frozen goods would melt. So, I opened the ice cream to check it. It tasted so good, that I finished the whole container before finishing my work with the tire.

5. The architect called to see if the plans were completed. He/she needs them for the presentation tomorrow. If the dimensions are not correct, then, revisions will be necessary. There is not enough time for major revisions, however. We created the plans using the specifications given to us.

6. The receptionist advised me that a woman was waiting to see me. When I was ready to meet with her, the receptionist brought her to my office. I motioned for her to sit in the chair across from me and asked her for information about the case. She disclosed that she was cheating on her husband and wanted to leave him. I explained the divorce filing process to her. She decided that she would consider our discussion before finalizing her decision to start the divorce proceedings.

7. "Quiet! You have the right to remain silent, anything that you say can and will be used against you in a court of law." As the officer finished mirandizing the criminal, he noticed three men approaching. The officer waited warily as the men came closer, wondering if they would attack. Not wanting to risk an altercation, the officer worked quickly to secure the criminal in the cruiser. After starting the car, the group passed without incident. Breathing a sigh of relief, the officer wondered if it was time to schedule a vacation!

8. Excitedly, the group of students discussed graduation plans. They discussed their future career goals and present job searches. One woman announced that she would start a new job working in an animation studio beginning next Monday. Another woman commented that she was still attending interviews to work as a legal assistant. Two men, both graduating with honors, stated that they were going to start a consulting business together. All concluded that they could not wait to use their experience and education in new careers.

9. Someone called to complain that <u>he/she</u> does have not have power in <u>his/her</u> house. Before we send a team of linemen to the area, can <u>you</u> check to see if there are other reported outages? Please check the grid for that area and report back to <u>me</u>.

10. Please check the gaskets to see if they still fit tightly. If <u>it</u> is not coming from there, then try to follow the leak through the engine. Look for the areas that have the most oil, <u>you</u> will find the source of the leak.

EXERCISE 10.4: Student answers will vary for this section. Be certain that the sentences are written more specifically so that "this, that, it, these, and those" are replaced.

EXERCISE 10.5:

1. I

2. herself

3. We

4. we, I

5. me

6. himself

7. they

8. She

9. them, us

10. she, I

11. myself

12. they

13. we, ourselves

14. yours

15. we, our

16. him, me

17. her, herself

18. She, I, we, ourselves

19. itself

20. we

Chapter 11: Word Usage

TROUBLESOME WORDS AND HOMONYMS

EXERCISE 11.1:

1. Currently, (they're, their, <u>there</u>) is no licensing of paralegals in any state.

2. Notice (to, <u>too</u>, two), that when specifying the rotation angle, the original orientation of the selected object is taken to be 0 degrees.

3. When the camshaft is installed, you (than, <u>then</u>) coat the lobes with a special lubricant.

4. If (your, <u>you're</u>) a crime victim, (you're, <u>your</u>) rights have been violated.

5. Strips of boxing wax are used to form a rim around an impression (that, <u>which</u>) contains the poured gypsum material.

6. The department's goal is (two, <u>to</u>, too) put all of (it's, <u>its</u>) aircraft manuals on CD-ROM.

7. By using larger cells, (that, <u>which</u>) have a larger quantity of material, the ability to supply current can be increased but the voltage is not (<u>affected</u>, effected).

8. For risk diagnosis, (now, <u>no</u>, know) subjective and objective signs are present.

9. The difference in energy levels is (quiet, <u>quite</u>, quit) smaller (then, <u>than</u>) the difference in energy between shells.

10. People collect data and information because they expect it to be useful later, (<u>whether</u>, weather) to identify drivers, to diagnose and treat medical problems, or to train employees.

11. A developmental pathologic condition (that, <u>which</u>) can (effect, <u>affect</u>) the teeth is anodontia.

12. A prisoner's sentence can be reduced (thorough, threw, <u>through</u>, thru) parole.

13. To (insure, <u>ensure</u>) proper electrical connection (<u>to</u>, too, two) the inflator module in the steering wheel, a coil assembly is used in the steering column.

14. Drawing an isometric (plain, <u>plane</u>) in AutoCAD is an advanced skill.

15. (Its, <u>It's</u>) necessary to determine (weather, <u>whether</u>) the location is appropriate before asking for a change of venue.

16. If (you're, <u>your</u>) combinations of viewpoints are associated with one another, you can group them into a viewpoint configuration for easy redisplay.

17. If (their, there, <u>they're</u>) lightly scored, the clearances in the pump should be measured.

18. The law is like a living thing (that, <u>which</u>) (<u>affects</u>, effects) change over time.

19. Many companies have (they're, <u>their</u>, there) own local or regional training (sights, cites, <u>sites</u>) designed to train beginning service technicians and to provide update training (four, <u>for</u>, fore) existing technicians.

20. You will be able to rotate the (plain, <u>plane</u>) of your model so that you can see (you're, <u>your</u>) model as you change (<u>your</u>, you're) view of it.

21. You can (excess, <u>access</u>) the command by typing it on the command line.

22. The last tool generates camera views (<u>which</u>, that) is explained (farther, <u>further</u>) in later chapters.

23. The employer for (<u>whom</u>, who) the paralegal works must (except, <u>accept</u>) ultimate responsibility and accountability for the work of the legal assistant in his or her office.

24. Most large dealerships employ service technicians (that, which, <u>who</u>) are highly skilled.

25. Expert witnesses must demonstrate their expertise (thru, thorough, threw, <u>through</u>) education, work experience, publications, and awards.

26. A caustic substance (<u>that</u>, which) comes in contact with the eyes is (quit, quiet, <u>quite</u>) serious; if it happens, flush (you're, <u>your</u>) eyes with water immediately, (<u>then</u>, than) seek medical attention as quickly as possible.

27. As you (now, <u>know</u>, no), (its, <u>it's</u>) common practice to exchange business cards the first time you meet someone.

28. When (they're, <u>there</u>) is no coil current, the armature is held against the upper contact by the spring (<u>that</u>, which) provides continuity from terminal 1 to terminal 2.

29. The nurse administers medication to the patient (that, <u>who</u>, which) is in need of it, (than, <u>then</u>) records the action on the chart.

30. Assessment of the abdomen involves (fore, for, <u>four</u>) methods of examination: inspection, auscultation, palpation, and percussion.

SLANG AND COLLOQUIAL EXPRESSIONS

EXERCISE 11.2: The answers given below are examples of how some students may answer. Since slang words have different meanings for people, student answers will vary.

1. The supervisor called me last night to ask me to come to work because the company's computer system **suffered a malfunction**!

2. We are so **excited** by the news that the hospital will add more per diem medical assistant shifts; we will be able to earn more money.

3. I waited for **you** to return my call before calling local shops for a used crankshaft.

4. I don't understand why he was **so upset** yesterday when, I clearly followed the arrest procedure.

5. **Is something bothering you**? We needed your help with the rewiring of the house.

6. The new program arrived today. **I am very excited**!

7. How **much money** do you want for the lumber?

8. "**See you later**," screamed Evelyn as she exited the building.

9. Our instructor was **understanding** about our assignments being handed in late.

10. Hank is **excited** that the school superintendent accepted his bid to design the new elementary school.

11. It **bothers** me when the other legal assistants forget to return the law books to the proper shelves.

12. I realized that since I was promoted to detective in our department, everyone **comments that I spend a lot of time behind my desk**.

13. He acts **so arrogantly** around our shop; I can't stand it.

14. The food served at our boss's party was **delicious**.

15. After working all night, Ellen went home to **sleep** before having to report back to the police station.

16. Rather than losing her temper all the time, she really needs to **relax**.

17. I heard that the other technician is **emotional**; too bad you have to work with her.

18. The hospital where we completed our internship is **dilapidated**.

19. Have you seen his new **vehicle**? I hear that the car used to be a mess, but now, it is in **excellent condition**!

20. Yesterday's meeting was so **strange**; the client said that our work was **well-done**.

1. I think that perhaps, she is mentally deficient.

2. He reported that he is ecstatic.

3. She is very tall and thin.

4. If you do not complete this project, you are endangering your position here.

5. Martha reminded us that we had better not be ungrateful.

6. Do not make hasty judgments.

7. No matter how stubborn someone else is, you cannot make him agree with you.

8. This house is so noisy that I cannot get any rest.

9. I do not understand how that statement relates to our conversation.

10. He talks too much.

Bibliography

The bibliography below includes those texts used as either general or specific reference material for this manual. In certain exercises, specific sentences were taken directly from the listed texts.

Adkins, Jeanette. *The Prentice Hall Grammar Workbook.* Upper Saddle River, New Jersey: Prenctice Hall 2003.

Andujo, Emily. *Prentice Hall Health Complete Review: Dental Assisting.* USR, NJ: Prentice Hall, 2004.

Arlov, Pamela. *Wordsmith: A Guide to Paragraphs and Short Essays*, 2nd ed. USR, NJ: Prentice Hall, 2004.

_____. *Wordsmith: A Guide to College Writing.* 2nd ed. USR, NJ: Prentice Hall, 2004.

Arlov, Panela and Nick Arlov. *Wordsmith: Essentials of College English (Instructor's Edition).* USR, NJ: Prentice Hall, 2004.

Davis, Deborah. *The Adult Learner's Companion: A Guide to Student Success* (Tentative Title). Boston: Houghton Mifflin, 2006.

Dix, Mark and Paul Riley. *Discovering AutoCAD 2004.* USR, NJ: Prentice Hall, 2004.

Ethier, Stephen J. and Christine A. Ethier. *AutoCAD in 3 Dimensions Using AutoCAD 2004.* USR, NJ: Prentice Hall, 2004.

Floyd, Thomas L. *Electronics Fundamentals: Circuits, Devices, and Applications.* 6th ed. USR, NJ: Prentice Hall, 2004.

Goodrich, David Lee. *The Basics of Paralegal Studies.* USR, NJ: Prentice Hall, 2004.

Halderman, James D. and Chase D. Mitchell, Jr. *Automotive Technology: Principles, Diagnosis, and Service.* 2nd ed. USR, NJ: Prentice Hall, 2003.

Kozier, Barbara, et al. *Fundamentals of Nursing: Concepts, Process, and Practice.* 7th ed. USR, NJ: Prentice Hall, 2004.

Lannon, John M. *Technical Writing.* 6th ed. New York: HarperCollins College Publishers, 1994.

Senn, James A. *Information Technology: Principles, Practices, Opportunities.* 3rd ed. USR, NJ: Prentice Hall, 2004.

Schmalleger, Frank. *Criminal Justice Today: An Introductory Text for the 21st Century (Annotated Instructor's Edition).* 8th ed. USR, NJ: Prentice Hall, 2005.

10. Writing good college papers requires knowing what the teacher wants, good grammar skills, and strong organizational skills.

    a. I have to know what the teacher wants before I write a paper, so I need to know

    _____.

    b. I know I can improve my grammar skills to write a better paper if I

    _____.

    c. Paying attention to organization in my college writing will help me to

    _____.

Transitional Phrases

Transitional phrases are those words and phrases which contribute to the paper's coherence. These phrases provide strong, solid connections between ideas and paragraphs. Transitional words act as signposts, direct the reader where you want him to go. Without them, the paper lacks unity and coherence.

❧ *EXERCISE 1.9* ❧

Using the ten sentences below, add the appropriate transitional word or phrase to help the reader understand what you're saying. For example,

I know that my own study space is essential for my success. I can create my own study space by finding a place in my house I can call my own, one that is used solely for studying, and allows for necessary privacy.

        a. <u>First</u> (transitional word), I need to have a space that is all mine, not my family's, just mine.

        b. <u>In addition</u> (transitional words), I need a study place that is used exclusively for studying.

        c. <u>Finally</u> (transitional word), I need privacy for efficient studying.

1. For me, attending college will offer me the opportunity to advance my career, secure a better paying job, and be a role model for my children.

    a. Going to college will help me in my career by _____.

    b. I know a college degree will improve my chances to make a better salary by

    _____.

    c. By going to college, my children_____.

5. In preparing for a test, I need to study several days before the test, meet with my study group, and know what will be on the test.
   a. The benefits of studying several days before the test, versus cramming the night before include _____.
   b. My study group can help me prepare for a test by_____
   _____.
   c. I need to know what will be on the test so that I can _____
   _____.

6. I know that to study efficiently, I need to create my own study place, have privacy, and regulate my study times.
   a. By creating my own study area, I can _____.
   b. Privacy when I study will help me to _____.
   c. Setting specific study times will allow me to _____.

7. To make the most out of my college education, I need to communicate with the staff, get to know my faculty advisor, and learn about my program in the college catalogue.
   a. The college staff can help me to _____.
   b. I need to know my faculty advisor because_____.
   c. The more familiar I am with the college catalogue, the more _____
   _____.

8. It's so difficult to meet new people in college. Sometimes I feel self-conscious, like no one will understand me, and that I'm so different.
   a. My being self-conscious makes me _____.
   b. I don't think any of these students will understand me because _____
   _____.
   c. I'm not like any of these students. I'm _____.

9. Taking effective notes in class will help me to better prepare for tests, understand the material, and develop my listening skills.
   a. I know the teacher asks questions on tests based on her lectures. If I take better notes, I can _____.
   b. Reviewing my notes from class helps me understand the material the teacher discussed, so taking good notes _____.
   c. Listening is so important, especially in class. It_____
   _____.

2. I'm trying to learn the skills of time management; it's a difficult task because of my many responsibilities such as work, raising my children, and going to school.

  a. Managing my time is hard with my work schedule which _____ _____.

  b. Not only does work take time, but my children _____ _____.

  c. Budgeting my time includes school which _____.

3. My goal, once I get my degree, is to own my own business, so that I can be financially independent, be my own boss, and make my family proud.

  a. With my own business, I can _____.

  b. Financial independence will allow me to _____.

  c. As the owner of my own business, my family _____ _____.

4. I'd like to learn how to reduce my stress because my blood pressure is too high, my temper flares up, and I'm not sleeping well.

  a. My high blood pressure due to stress makes my body _____ _____.

  b. When I'm really stressed, my temper _____.

  c. Because of stress, I'm not sleeping well, so I _____ _____.

5. In preparing for a test, I need to study several days before the test, meet with my study group, and know what will be on the test.

  a. The benefits of studying several days before the test, versus cramming the night before include _____.

  b. My study group can help me prepare for a test by _____ _____.

  c. I need to know what will be on the test so that I can _____ _____.

6. I know that to study efficiently, I need to create my own study place, have privacy, and regulate my study times.

  a. By creating my own study area, I can _____.

  b. Privacy when I study will help me to _____.

  c. Setting specific study times will allow me to _____.

⟨ *EXERCISE 1.9* ⟩

Using the ten sentences below, add the appropriate transitional word or phrase to help the reader understand what you're saying. For example,

> **I know that my own study space is essential for my success. I can create my own study space by finding a place in my house I can call my own, one that is used solely for studying, and allows for necessary privacy.**
>
> a. <u>First</u> (transitional word), I need to have a space that is all mine, not my family's, just mine.
>
> b. <u>In addition</u> (transitional words), I need a study place that is used exclusively for studying.
>
> c. <u>Finally</u> (transitional word), I need privacy for efficient studying.

1. For me, attending college will offer me the opportunity to advance my career, secure a better paying job, and be a role model for my children.

   a. Going to college will help me in my career by _____.

   b. I know a college degree will improve my chances to make a better salary by

      _____.

   c. By going to college, my children _____.

14